Mel

You are

awesome

UNSTOPPABLE LIFE

by
Stuart Ellis-Myers
a.k.a.
Twitchy

If a man living with the rare
neurological disorder Tourettes Syndrome
can become a happily married keynote speaker and author
... then what is holding you back from achieving your dreams?

First Edition trade paperback - 2015 Uniquely Speaking, Inc

For information about special discounts for bulk purchases please contact doris@itwitch.com or 1 604 709 4446 or visit www.itwitch.com

Speaker Bureau
To book Stuart to keynote perform at your next live event please contact doris@itwitch.com call 1 604 709 4446 or visit www.itwitch.com

Design by Stuart Ellis-Myers and Motiontide Media, Inc

Canadian Cataloguing First Publication Date: May 2015

ISBN-13: 978-0-9868781-8-3
E-Book ISBN: 978-0-9868781-9-0

Stuart Ellis-Myers

UNSTOPPABLE

1. Self-help   2. Business   3. Autobiography   4. Personal Growth

ABOUT THE AUTHOR

Stuart Ellis-Myers is an inspiring model of courage and determination. When he speaks of improving lives, he does so from the perspective of painful personal experience.

In spite of struggling with the hardships of a dysfunctional family, brutal childhood bullying, and the ravages of one of the most misunderstood mental conditions – Tourettes Syndrome – he has gone on to become an Internationally renowned and highly respected Keynote Speaker.

In demand by major associations and corporations from all over the world, he delivers thoughtful, yet dynamic, presentations on subjects critical to creating a successful business in these challenging times, such as: Sales, Customer Relations, Communication, Leadership, and developing Unstoppable Management Practices.

For many years, Stuart has delivered his experientially directed message of empowerment and self-determination to thousands of individuals, in countless meeting rooms and conference facilities. Now, he brings that same "turning weakness into strength" message to you, through the pages of this book.

It is Stuart's heartfelt hope that you will be able to gain insight and inspiration from his story and that you will find encouragement in those lessons he has learned and is sharing with you on these pages.

An Unstoppable life begins with a first step. Perhaps this is yours.

For Doris, the love of my life

CONTENTS

ACKNOWLEDGEMENTS

I would like to thank a few of the people who have contributed to both this book and the life that inspired it.

To my dearest Mother and my "true" Father, I wish to thank you for the constant, never-ending, unconditional love that you have showered upon your twitchy child. You are amazing parents and I will never be able to adequately express either my gratitude, or my love to you.

To my Australian family – Bob, Took, Jules and Andy – for being there when I was completely "down under". You believed in me, when I no longer believed in myself.

To Stephen Maxworthy, Nada Jenkins and Estrellita Gonzales, you will always be my brother and sisters – by choice.

To my mentors, Stephan Huesing and George Kennedy, you taught me to see the potential in others, even when they did not see it in themselves. You both left this world too soon and we are poorer for it.

To Peter and Sandra Bibby, if not for you, I would not even be here. Your steadfast and unquestioning support and encouragement through those dark and hopeless days, still brings tears of gratitude and love to my eyes. You saved me. I can only hope that I make you proud of having done so.

To George and Joan Pitman, Issa and Susan Nahkleh, Joe Smith & family, Shaun and Kelly Huswouk, Geoffy and Barb Last and Sal and Dick, you all know why and believe me when I tell you how important you all are to me.

To George Milman, the coolest guy in the world, and to Michael Novak, without whom this book could have never been possible.

To Doris, the love of my life and the mate of my soul. You are my rock, my North Star, my solace and my joy. Without you, the light would not shine as brilliantly.

And, finally, to all of the bullies of my youth. Without you, I might never have learned just how strong I really am. Your torment and your torture became the crucible in which my resolve was formed. I now understand your pain and fear. I forgive you and I hope that you can forgive those who made you feel small and frightened. Please do not allow the darkness of your past to destroy the bright future you can still have.

FOREWORD

There's all the difference in the world between surviving and thriving. Through fear, inertia, lack of confidence in ourselves, many of us spend a lot of time on the 'surviving' end of the spectrum. It takes self-awareness, courage and an awful lot of persistence to swim upstream and reach 'thriving'. And even more hard work to stay there. Stuart Ellis-Myers isn't a survivor. He's a thriver. Yes, I know it's not a proper word, but how else to describe Stuart: someone who's looked at his past, looked deeply within, and decided that he can be whomever he wants to be and achieve whatever he wants to achieve. That he's going to be Unstoppable.

Stuart is unflinching in sharing his challenges as well as his success. Some challenges he's put behind him, and others he lives with every day. He enjoys his success, but doesn't ever take it for granted. He shares his story because he believes that by describing his journey and the struggle to find his path, he may help you to seek and find your own. Because you can be Unstoppable too.

Lynn
Lynn McLarnon
Executive Director

Tourette Canada

"Balls! Bitch! Pussy! Cock!"

I twitch. I jerk. I shriek.
I cluck. I moan. I grunt.
I hop. I tick. I gesture wildly.
I am compelled to knock my elbow three times.
Not four ... three.

Welcome to my life. If you take a look at what I do – as I have outlined above – you might be excused for thinking that I am more than a little crazy. I am not. I merely have Tourettes Syndrome.

Tourettes Syndrome (TS) is a neurological disorder characterized by involuntary movements and vocalizations. It is in many ways different for each of us who struggle to cope with TS.

In my case, I have a delightful variety of twitches, including: eye blinking, odd facial movement and shoulder shrugging. Oh, and my head and shoulders jerk entirely at random. If that wasn't enough, I also vocalize constantly. Strange tones, grunting sounds, repetitive throat clearing and sniffing. Fortunately for me ... I don't swear. (The opening statement reflects my attitude, not my affliction.)

In addition, most of us who suffer from TS also live with high levels of anxiety, panic attacks, and depression. We are often Bipolar. Throw in Attention Deficit Disorder (ADD) and Obsessive Compulsive Disorder (OCD) and then add in all of the socialization issues we have developed over the years, as our response to your response to us.

According to the World Health Organization, I have about four hundred and fifty million brothers and sisters who live with some type of mental disorder. We all struggle to make it through each day of our lives. Some of us fail.

Sadly, far too many people living with mental health issues end up unemployed, addicted to alcohol or drugs, divorced and isolated. Virtually "thrown away" by society.

On the other hand, there are many of us who have been able to build happy, fulfilling and successful lives. I am one of those ... and this is why I have written this book.

The simple message I offer in this book, is this:

If I can overcome everything you have just read, and everything you are about to read, and go on to build a life of both personal and professional success ... what is stopping you?

If you are still reading this, you probably want to know just how I managed to pull off this particular miracle. You might also want to know if what I have learned on my journey will be of any aid to you on yours.

It can. It should. In fact, it already has helped many people from all different backgrounds, with their own different problems; find greater success at work and greater joy in their private lives.

In some strange way, I am grateful for what I have had to endure.

Thanks to Tourettes, I was forced early in life to learn to overcome a lot of problems that "normal" people never have to face. Unlike you, my constant twitching and grimacing made it impossible for me to hide my weaknesses away. People noticed. Boy did they ever! Especially the bullies. Their "attention" forced me to look within for the strengths that I now know lie hidden away in all of us.

Perhaps this is the time to find these strengths and move beyond your own self-diagnosed (and self-enforced) limitations.

What I will share with you here, is the story of my journey and how I finally discovered that all of the strengths I was desperately seeking, were in fact hidden away in what I had been taught to consider my weakness.

There are many who would consider what I do every day to be impossible. One of the greatest fears that the average person suffers, is that of having to speak in public. There was even a study, a few years ago, that stated that most people would rather have surgery than speak to a group of people, and yet that is what I do almost every day of my life. I am, in fact, the only Keynote speaker in the world who suffers from Tourettes.

So, how did I get from being the sad, lonely, badly bullied child who twitched, and jerked, and moaned, and just generally freaked everybody out ... to being the capable, competent, successful, happily married minor celebrity that I am today? Well, it starts with this:

My definition of *insanity*, is people who waste their lives away in needless frustration, foolishly waiting for that perfect moment to arrive when they will be set free to live the life they have always dreamed of.

My definition of *madness*, is choosing, perhaps even preferring, to hide away your true self in fear of the disapproval of others.

My definition of *crazy*, is standing back and watching people fail to realize that everything they need to succeed is already within them.

From my "twitchy" perspective, it is nothing short of lunacy to put up with living less than a full and happy life.

If you are like virtually everyone I have ever met, you possess an infinite number of truly amazing talents, that are just sitting there waiting for you to wake up and use them.

However, you are probably also like most of those lovely people, in that you hesitate to do so. You hold back, you hesitate, you turn away from the challenge and, as a result, you remain disconnected from the life you should be living. It is as if an invisible, but irresistible, force is holding you back from reaching for your dreams.

Perhaps you believe that you are helpless to change your life for the better. That you are overwhelmed by an impossible set of circumstances, that you feel you can barely survive let alone overcome.

You are not alone in this. I have been exactly where you are. In many ways, I still am. Thanks to my Tourettes, my never ending depression, my ADD, my OCD, and my often near crippling anxiety, I begin each new day facing issues that seem impossible to overcome.

It is here that I make the choice. Despair and hopelessness are always options, but there are also other choices available to me, to all of us.

The choice I make every morning, is to live my life to the fullest. To get the most out of everything I do, and to learn the most from everyone I meet. I also try to share. My time. My talents. My love.

It is in that spirit, that I write this book. These pages exist to share how I was able to create an "unstoppable" life.

Perhaps my insights, and the actions I have used to turn the disabilities that threatened to render my life one of misery and failure, into the abilities that have taken me around the world and filled my life with joy and love, will help you to take the first/next step toward your own **Unstoppable Life**.

CHAPTER 1
Everyone is someone's fool

It was a wonderful day. Sunny, warm, a gentle breeze filled with the promise of a beautiful evening soon to come. Doris, my amazing wife, and I had just spent more time than you would think possible shopping at a local organic farm. Loaded up with blueberries and green beans, we were walking to our car – holding hands like high school sweethearts – when it all changed.

There was a small boy who had wandered away from his family. I am not good with children's ages, but I guessed that he could not have been much older than two or three. Now, I know that trying to raise children in today's world is challenging, but I found what was happening to be difficult to watch.

For the record, he had only gone about twenty feet from where they were standing and he was in clear sight and in no danger whatsoever. Still, his mother reacted as if the world was coming to an end. She grabbed him by the hand and, with her face only inches from his, started to tell him about all the terrible things that could happen to him if he ever left her side again.

Obviously, I know that this is a scene that is repeated just about everywhere, pretty much all the time, but it really struck home with me at that moment. It immediately took me back to my own childhood and I realized – maybe for the first time – that all of my fears had been given to me by others.

Some by schoolyard bullies, some by total strangers, some by family, some – and these were the hardest to bear – by those I loved and thought loved me.

We are not born to fear, it is something we learn. Something we are taught. We carry the fear we learn as children for the rest of our lives and, while we cannot change our past, we must not allow these fears to stop us from changing our future.

Some time ago, I was on a flight out of Tel Aviv, Israel. I had just finished giving the Keynote address at Israel's National Tourism Leaders conference, to over 500 tourism professionals, and I was on my way to Houston to speak at a major Pharmaceutical conference.

Now, I am not just bragging here, this is my life. This is what I do and, as we climbed into the sky over the Mediterranean, I closed my eyes and began to reflect on how fortunate, and how grateful, I was to even be on this flight, let alone to have this job, this life.

Truth be told, if you had asked me twenty years ago, "What do you see yourself doing in the future?" it certainly would not have been this. It would not have even been close to this. The sorry fact of the matter, is that most people like me, living with this rare and sadly misunderstood neurological disorder, spend their days in overwhelming anxiety and crippling depression.

Many live marginal lives of poverty and despair. According to most of what I have read on this subject, I should not be accomplished, successful and happily married. Instead, I should be divorced, alone, unemployed, socially marginalized, possibly even homeless.

So, why am I sitting here in First Class, instead of sleeping in a dumpster?

Why am I successful, fulfilled and, dare I even say it, happy? It was a choice. It wasn't an easy one to make, and it was harder still to accomplish, but here indeed I am. And here I will stay. Not in spite of my many challenges, but because of them.

All of us come to an emotional crossroad in our lives. In fact, we come to many of them. This is where we get to make the choices that govern our lives. We can choose to deny that we are weak, that we are fearful, that we have any problems at all . . . certainly any that we can do anything about. Or we can do the incredibly heavy lifting required and choose to stop lying to ourselves and take the first steps to learning how to start taking chances.

To face our fears and overcome them. To come out of each new failure with boundless enthusiasm for the next challenge. Just like me, it is possible for anyone to learn how to hop, skip, and even merrily twitch over so many of the barriers we are all told, over and over and over again, that we cannot possibly overcome.

We do not have to remain as small children, standing crying in a parking lot, being taught to fear by those who learned it from someone else. We can wipe our tears, pull up our big kid pants, and just get on with it.

For most of my life, I simply assumed that the answers I was looking for existed somewhere outside myself. I don't know why I thought this. Perhaps it was just something I had learned from others who felt that they had no direct and personal control over their lives.

I had become another of those lost souls who believe that if I waited long enough, or prayed hard enough, or read enough of the right kind of books, or hung around the right kind of people, or . . . whatever, then one day the answers would magically appear and my life would be glorious. Well, it didn't happen that way. Not even a little bit.

Instead, it was a slow, gradual, even painful process of enlightenment. I learned to try to do something, anything, even when everyone else told me it was impossible for anyone to achieve, especially someone like me.

Perhaps the hardest thing I had to do was break free of my own "prison of sorrows", that place where all of my unresolved issues and past traumatic experiences lived, and step into the terrifying world of change.

Change is one of the most frightening things in life. For much of my life, I chose to life my life imprisoned by my fears because, however damaging, they were also comfortable. I knew them and I had learned to live whatever life I could within their confines.

Still, I was not happy. I am not sure I really knew what that meant. Oh sure, there were times, moments, when I felt good about myself, but those were few and far between. I guess that I had simply come to accept that this was my life and it was as good as it was going to get. After all, as I had so frequently been reminded, what more could someone like me expect?

Well, that has changed. I am not that guy anymore. Okay, I am still basically that guy; I didn't actually become someone else; but I don't let my past determine my future anymore. And neither should you.

I see so many people, with truly amazing talents and abilities, choosing to deny their true potential and hide themselves away in their own prison of sorrows. It breaks my heart to see them, looking at their lives in the dark and dirty looking glass of negativity and self-doubt.

Look, if someone like me can do this, anyone can. I was, for much of my life, painfully introverted and constantly anxious. Today, I stand alone on stages around the world, speaking to hundreds of people at a time, helping others to find their own paths to becoming Unstoppable.

If someone like me, once depressed and fearful and filled with self-doubt, can now wake up every morning next to the woman of my dreams, happily married and constantly aware of the joys of my life, then so too can anyone.

I recently returned home after a long business trip, exhausted, ready for a hot bath and a cold beer, wanting nothing more than some quiet time with my darling wife. I walked into our lovely little home and found it jammed to the walls with my dearest friends, people I love and who genuinely love me.

I had forgotten it was my birthday, but they had not. They had come together to celebrate me. To show how much they valued my being in their lives. As joyous as the occasion was, it did remind me that, for much of my life, I wasn't all that sure that I valued it.

The rest of you non-twitchy people out there can easily hide your fears and weaknesses away from casual observation. Tourettes afforded me no such luxury. My mind and body betrayed me on a constant basis. I could not hide my fears. I could not even understand, let alone overcome, my weaknesses.

I was only eight years old when it began. The urge to twitch and constantly gesture. The irrepressible need to vocalize in surprisingly unsociable, and obviously unacceptable, ways. It took a very long time before I even knew what it was that was happening to me and even then I did not fully understand it.

For the longest time, I believed that living with Tourettes was going to be impossible. In addition, thanks to Bipolar Disorder being an imbedded trait of Tourettes, I lived with a deep and abiding sense of never ending despair. At my worst, it felt as if my life was walking on broken glass and chewing razor blades for lunch.

At its best, it felt like my life – at any moment – was going to come to an entirely horrible end. I knew that I could not continue to live like this. Who could? So, I decided it was time to do something about it. The solution seemed pretty clear. I would simply kill myself and then it would be done.

The thought of suicide paid me a visit when I was in my early thirties. On paper, my life looked pretty good. Happily married. Check! Hopelessly in love. Check! Successful career. Check! My life was wonderful, except it actually wasn't. I learned that day, that everyone is someone's fool. On that particular day, it was me.

My wife, who (along with *almost* everyone else I will mention in this book) shall remain nameless, came home that evening and told me it was over. One moment I was blissfully happy, floating in the fluffy clouds of never ending love, and the next I was shot out of the sky by a "happiness seeking" rocket of cold and brutal betrayal. That might have sounded a little melodramatic, but it turned out to be fairly accurate.

It seems that she had never really loved me and that our four year marriage had been a huge mistake. It hit me that she and her family had spent the better part of the last year planning her departure.

Nobody, it seemed, wanted any part of me being her husband and certainly not the father of any children, who would most certainly be born with my many terrible afflictions. That is not how it works, by the way, but nobody had thought to ask me. Understandable, I suppose, but despicable nonetheless.

I begged her to stay. She didn't. I told her I would get over her. I didn't. What I did do, was unravel like a cheap scarf. To say that I fell to pieces, would be to understate it in the extreme. My nightmares of anger and regret soon brought on three months of insomnia.

I lost sixty pounds, living on a diet of milk and cigarettes. I was a physical and emotional wreck. I was done. Enough was enough. It was time to bring this misery to an end and I knew just how to do it. I was going to die and then everything would be fine. Just fine.

Except for one thing. I really didn't want to upset my mother. I mean, she is very nice lady. This would be a horribly mean thing to do to her. She would be devastated. I couldn't do that to her. I also couldn't go on living like I had been doing. Great . . . so now what?

Well, first I started to cry. Then I started to laugh. Then I started to do . . . I actually don't remember what I did then, but finally, I started to think. And, I've got to tell you . . . it sucked. I was finally forced to look at my life and see it for what it was and not some fantasy I had quite deliberately tortured into existence. At that moment, I knew – beyond a shadow of a doubt – that something did have to die. Not me. It was my old life that had to go.

Standing at the edge of the dark and cold abyss that is suicide, I knew that one of us was doomed. Either it was the end of my old life, or it would be the end of me. The choice wasn't as easy as you might think. This life was all I knew. Who would I be now?

I was totally and hopelessly lost. And that is what saved me. It was here at the lowest point in my life, knowing that I had lost everything that mattered to me, that I realized I simply did not have anything else to lose.

In that moment, I just let go. I let go of the fears I had been taught by others. I let go of the regrets I had been hoarding. I let go of all of the decisions I had made, that had brought me to this moment, and I forgave myself for all of the mistakes and the bad choices and the total lack of perfection that defined my life.

I tossed my old life into the darkness and started forward with a clean sheet of paper. This new life was going to be of my own, better, honest design.

In that stunning moment of truly letting go, I began to finally hear a new voice. One that actually turned out to be an old one. It was mine. I had not heard it for a very long time, but now it was crystal clear. It was loud and it had something to say. A lot to say. And, finally, I was ready to listen.

It encouraged me to look at the pieces of my life, the ones lying broken and scattered on the floor around me, and choose the ones that would fit together in this new life I was building. One of better choices. One of self-determination, no longer subject to the fears of my past and the errors of my pathology.

One of courage and strength and commitment and forgiveness. I looked back at all of the influences in my life. The schoolyard bullies who tormented me mercilessly. My parents, trapped in a loveless marriage, bound more by fear than devotion. Even my soon to be ex-wife and the dilemma of her trying to find the perfect husband. These were the emotional chains I had been dragging through my old life and they had no place in my new one.

So, what did belong in my new life? Well, I took that clean sheet of paper and I started to write down what I knew absolutely to be true about myself:

I was born to be on a stage.

My constant bullying as a child, had taught me to be resilient. At the very least, it had taught me to overcome the more common forms of rejection.

As a result of the never ending challenges of living with Tourettes, I had inadvertently learned how to never give in. I had learned to go from failure to failure with great enthusiasm. All I had to do now, was learn to go from failure to success.

Most of all, I knew, almost instinctively, that if I could somehow make it in this new life, if I could learn how to overcome and deal with my inner madness, then I could also learn to help others with their own everyday outer world madness.

I began to become very excited. Only minutes before I was filled with sadness and despair, now I was filled with hope and the joy of new challenges, new choices. Just by choosing to walk away from the darkness, without anything from my old life, I was able to step forward into what felt like the brightest of light.

That feeling has never left me. I feel it each and every day. If anything, as I am more able to help and serve others, it is becoming even stronger. Each time someone comes up to me after one of my presentations and tells me how the light just went on for them, I am filled with unmitigated joy for the changes that have occurred in my life.

For the ways in which I can now help others to navigate through the labyrinths of doubt and fear that plague us all. To help them find that place to stand, where the restrictive rules, and the crippling fears, and the dreams and hopes that have been shattered through the years, can quickly and effectively be taken from them.

You might notice that I did not say "easily". Quickly? Yes. Effectively? Sure. Easily? Not a chance.

I am not going to mislead you here. This is not easy. It will never be easy. But, boy is it worth it. Even at the point of wanting to kill myself, I knew that life was a magical gift.

At least, I knew that it could be. It was not something to be selfishly and stupidly thrown away. I realized, however, that there comes a time when you can no longer put up with all the pain and sorrow that surrounds you.

There is a tipping point, when your heart breaks and your soul rips open and you begin to realize that, for the longest time, it has been more painful to live than it seems to be to face the nothingness of death.

Looking back at that terrible moment, I can now see that instead of giving in or giving up, I made the conscious choice to no longer live by the rules that others had set out for me.

No longer was I going to play this game by someone else's rules. Especially when they virtually guaranteed that I did not have a fair chance of winning. No, from now on – win or lose – I was going to write my own rules.

CHAPTER 2

Writing your own rules

Looking back now, at that horrible/beautiful day, I can see that I made one of the most important choices of my life. I simply chose to no longer play by other people's rules and that changed everything.

Something miraculous happens when you start to write your own rules. In that instant, you finally take control of your life. Of course, you also take responsibility for it. Whatever happens – good and bad – is because you made the choice to take the control for your life into your own hands. Nobody and nothing is holding you back from being who you were truly meant to be. In so many ways, it is as if you get to start your life over again.

Even now, I can still feel the emotions of that day. The shift from misery and despair, to feelings of hope and confidence, filled me with the energy and commitment that allows me to start each new day with joy and enthusiasm.

If I am entirely truthful, I must thank Tourettes for giving me the stubbornness to stick around and get on with changing my life.

What I mean by that is simple; I knew that I had strength, after all I had spent my entire life fighting my way back from failure after failure; I knew that I had courage, after all I had spent my entire life standing up to the bullies who so delighted in my torment; I knew that I had commitment, after all I had been able to become successful in my career in spite of the crushing insecurity that was the cornerstone of my existence; I also knew that I was not living a life of my own choosing, I was living the life that had been chosen for me.

What I did not know, at that moment, was how much my very existence had been shaped by others. My head was constantly filled with the voices of those who had, whatever their true intentions, contributed to the life of sadness and regret mine had become.

I truly believe that each of us has to some degree created a "prison of sorrows", where we serve out our sentence. We have been put there by the judges of our past and kept there by the jailors of our future. The tragic fact of the matter, is that both the judges and the jailors are us. We have chosen to allow the harsh and strident voices of others to overwhelm the gentle and quiet voice that is our own.

When you finally make the choice to take control of your own life, you also become embarrassingly aware that is has been you, and only you, who is responsible for sabotaging your dreams and aspirations. You are the one who has been interfering with your own happiness and impeding your own success.

Strangely, once you recognize this, you feel kind of relieved. It is pretty simple really. If I am the one who has been holding me back, then all I have to do is turn around and start pushing me forward . . . right? If only it was that easy.

One of the basic Newtonian Laws of Physics is: for every action, there is an equal and opposite reaction. The same rules that apply to the physical world around us, also apply to the psychological world within. Every time we are pushed forward by our hopes and dreams, we are immediately pushed back by our doubts and fears. This is both perfectly natural and absolutely unavoidable. We have to do this.

There is a system of internal checks and balances that is simply human. These impulses helped our ancestors to both avoid being eaten by wild animals and yet inspired to create fire. The problem is when we allow ourselves to become trapped in this psychological shoving match.

When we allow the fearful chorus of negative voices in our heads to keep us trapped in limbo, we are lost. Even if it seems somehow safer to stick with the status quo, it will inevitably result in a smaller, less significant life.

I used to think that it was just people like me, with conditions like mine, who heard these voices. The Tourettes and the bipolar disorder were what was causing me to hear them. Normal people, healthy people, sane people didn't hear them. How could they? Why would they? And yet . . . they do.

We all do. In fact, most of us have become so used to hearing them, we no longer even try to do those things that trigger them. We have become all too willing to push our dreams and hopes and wishful plans for a better future, back into the dark and dingy corners of our consciousness simply to avoid cueing up the "choir of misery" that sits, oh so impatiently, waiting for us to try something we should already know we cannot do. It is actually quite comfortable there, in this safe haven of inertia. After all, you can't fail if you don't try anything new, anything different.

All of us know this feeling to some degree. Some of us more than others. We have become so accustomed to these voices, and their negative arguments against anything we have never tried before, that we rarely disagree with our initial, knee-jerk, reaction to any new and different challenge. It is often in these moments of greatest opportunity that we have the hardest time moving forward. We are, sadly, all too willing to trade the chance for a bigger and better future, for the safety of doing nothing. After all, if you don't try, you can't fail. Right?

The truth of the matter is, if you don't try . . . you have already failed.

Now, I am not saying that everything will work, every time you try something new. In fact, most things don't. There are literally countless ways for something to fail, and only a few ways for something to work. And, so what.

Failure doesn't make you a failure, quitting does. All failure means, is that you have not quite found the right way to succeed. Yet! The way to succeed is to keep trying. Learn from your failures. Make some changes. Try new things. Make choices. And write your own rules.

Bette Davis once said, that she would rather lose by her own rules than win by someone else's. I don't know if I would go quite that far, but I will admit to applauding the courage it takes to live that way. One of the beautiful things about writing your own rules, is that you truly own your success. Of course, you also own your many failures, but try to remember this; failure is only the middle of the story.

When you write your own rules, you can stop waiting for things to happen. You can start making them happen. So many of us have fallen into the habit of waiting for our lives to get good. We wait for that magical moment when the stars align and all the forces come together into the perfect situation when everything will work. We will surely be ready when that moment comes. You can count on it.

The only problem is, that moment just ain't coming. Not for me. Not for you. Not for anyone.

Now, it is your choice. If you want to, you can play by the rules you were taught. Be patient. Be quiet. Just sit there, shut up and wait. And wait. And wait. Something will happen . . . eventually.

And it will. You will die.

Seriously, if you want to keep relying on the fairy tales you were taught as a child, waiting for your fairy Godmother to arrive and wave her magic wand, making all of your dreams come true, then please dream on. It is your choice and I respect your right to make it.

But, if you actually want to turn your dreams into realities, you are going to have to get up off your butt, and way out of your comfort zone, and start writing some new rules.

All of us, at some point, will look back at our lives and wish that we could have/would have/should have done more with that life. Lived more, loved more, done more, been more. So, what is stopping us?

Most of us simply do not understand, that what is holding us back, is us. We abdicate the responsibility for the decisions we make. We refuse to listen to our own voice. We continue to live by other people's rules. And we suffer for it.

We do not, however, suffer silently. We talk about it all the time. Boy, do we ever. And what do we talk about? Mostly, for many of us, we talk about how everything will be different, once we win the lottery. We ransom our dreams, our hopes, our lives for a tiny piece of paper.

It doesn't seem to register, at least it doesn't seem to matter, that it is statistically more likely to be struck by lightning – twice – than it is to ever win a big lottery. The odds are millions to one that this could ever happen. But at least you are playing by the rules. Thiers's, of course.

Why, of course? Well, if you had made the rules, you wouldn't likely just be sitting there, waiting in vain, for your life to change.

If you were making the rules, you would be more likely to get up off your backside and formulate a real plan of action, based on your actual talents and abilities, to change your life.

And, by doing so, you would have changed the odds of success from millions to one, down to fifty/fifty. Either it will work, or it won't.

If it doesn't work, you learn from the experience, write a new rule, change the plan, and get on with it. Becoming unstoppable, means that every time we fail, we learn something new. This means that we can make a better plan. The knowledge that is gained from failure, is that which is vital to success.

Virtually all of the successful people I have ever met, spoken to, heard about, or read about, have failed at something. Many of them have failed at a lot of things. Over and over again. Yet they never quit.

Why not? Well, for one thing . . . it is against the rules.

Almost all successful people live their lives with one common rule. It is not a rule that the average person lives by. It is not a rule that most of us are taught. It is a rule that needs to be learned from within. What is that rule? If you have been paying attention, I mentioned it earlier. The rule is this . . . you can do anything but quit.

This was the first rule I made for myself, on that horrible/beautiful day. The day my new life, my true life, began.

The day I chose to turn away from the darkness and despair of my old life, and face the challenges and failures and successes of my new one.

So, what should be your first rule? I don't know, but you do.

CHAPTER 3

Avoiding the path of least resistance

In the previous chapter, I came down pretty hard on those of you who regularly purchase lottery tickets. I mean no disrespect, but it is important to, not just recognize what we do, but understand the reasons we do it. For many years, in my old life, I would purchase lottery tickets, but it was for a very different reason than you might think.

For months, I had been unable to sleep because I was obsessing about my job. I was in sales, a job most people with my affliction would go to great lengths to avoid. Someone with Tourettes, in a position of constantly dealing with the public, what kind of sense does that make?

It may not have made much sense, but it was my job and I was determined to do it well. Now, when I say "determined", obviously I mean "obsessed". It consumed my thoughts, especially when there was nothing else to distract me. Like when I was trying to go to sleep.

My solution was to place the cheapest lottery ticket I could buy under my pillow. I never checked to see if it was a winning ticket. That wasn't the point. Instead, if I couldn't sleep, I would place my hand under the pillow and touch the ticket.

Instantly, my scattered thoughts would focus. Instead of thoughts about failing at my job, I was driving down the California coast in a brand new Ferrari convertible, with a beautiful movie star by my side.

Or, I was flying my parents, in First Class of course, to see the brand new house I had built for them on some far and distant shore.

It really didn't matter what the fantasy was, it took me away from the fear and anxiety I was feeling about my life and allowed me to relax in a safe and comfortable place – of my own choosing – and drift blissfully off to sleep.

I used to tell myself that, while it might have all been nothing more than wishful thinking, at least it was better than alcohol or drugs. Except it wasn't.

The problem with depending on something outside of yourself for comfort or relief, is that the problems never actually go away. Nothing gets resolved. Sure, I was able to sleep at night, but when I woke up my life was still the same. I was the same twitchy, neurotic, unhappy mess I was the day before. Nothing had changed, least of all me.

So many of us, including the old me, want to have an amazing life, yet are unwilling to even begin to believe that we can get there under our own power. We are convinced that we have no control over the situation. We have been taught that, while some people might be able to do it (whatever it is), we most certainly can't.

Our families, our friends, our co-workers, pretty much everyone we know, is constantly saying to us, "You can't do that." What I have finally learned, is that what they are really saying is, "I can't do that." They are passing their fears, their insecurities, their rules on to us.

Let's give them the benefit of the doubt and assume that they are simply trying to protect you from failing at whatever it is they are trying to convince you not to do. Which is the worst possible thing they could do. You need to fail. Badly and often. Over and over again.

You have all watched babies try to walk. They stand up. They fall down. They stand up again. They fall down again. Until one day, they don't. They stay on their feet. They begin to move forward.

And a whole new world opens up for them. Just as it opens up for those of us who choose to try/fail/repeat. We stand up, fall down, write a new rule, and stand up again. Success is getting up one more time than having fallen down. Often success is nothing more than being the last person STANDING.

Is it hard? Sure. Is it scary? Often. Is it a risk? Always. So why do it? Why put yourself in that position? Because it works.

Talk to anyone who has become successful through their own efforts and they will talk about risk. How they had to put everything on the line, often more than once, to get where they are today. Success is no more an accident, than is failure. What?

Wait a minute . . . failure isn't an accident? Of course not. I am not going to get all Freudian on you here, but most accidents aren't. For example, you try something and it doesn't work. So, you tell yourself it was just the wrong place and the wrong time. An accident, right? Not even a little bit. After all, you chose the place, you chose the time.

What we need to do, is to stop looking at these moments as bad. Sure it is disappointing. It's frustrating, painful, embarrassing, and sad. But, it is also the absolute best thing in the world.

Whenever we try something new, something different, we are more likely to fail than succeed. We will fail over and over again.

Until, eventually, we don't. That is, if we have been paying attention to why we failed and make the changes to our plan to address the problem. Just doing the exact same thing over and over again, expecting a different result, has often been regarded as the true definition of insanity. Isn't that what got us into this mess in the first place? It certainly was for me. But, not anymore.

What I have learned, is something I already knew. Life in general, and learning to overcome these failures specifically, is pretty much like the lessons I learned from my early encounters with school yard bullies.

Just as I became a little stronger, each time I survived one of those events, we all become a little stronger each time we face our failures and our fears and make the necessary changes in our plans.

We return to the fray with the new and valuable insights, which can only be learned from falling flat on your face. Being unstoppable, is simply making the choice to get back up on your feet.

Maybe I was luckier than you. I learned very early on that giving in was not really an option for me. Kids, especially bullies, are merciless. I faced each new day, knowing that I was virtually guaranteed to be ridiculed and rejected. More often than not, I was also going to be punched and kicked.

I also knew that it was not going to stop, just because I wanted it to. The only possible way to put an end to all of this torture and torment, was to become invisible. So, what did I do?

I became an actor. I put myself as far out there as I possibly could. Looking back at it now, I don't really know why I did that. It seems to be the least likely thing for someone like me, especially the young me, to have done. It has been stated, that the average person would rather undergo surgery than speak in front of a room full of people. For an average person it is beyond difficult. For a twitchy, squeaky, awkward eight year old mess of a kid, it borders on mad.

As you can imagine, my teachers did not want to even audition me, let alone give me a role in any of the plays, but I was unstoppable. I auditioned for every role, in every play. Over and over again.

Eventually, I was given a part. I am sure it was more to make me go away, than it was because they thought I could do it. They were probably convinced that I would realize how terrible I was and quit. Only, I wasn't and I didn't.

They did everything they could to discourage me. At first I would have no lines, or only a few, and I would be stuck off to the side, or way in the back. It didn't matter to me. I was in the play. And the next one. And the one after that.

My breakthrough performance, was as Fabian in Shakespeare's "Twelfth Night". I still remember the day we were given the opportunity to audition for the play. I stood up at the front of the classroom, facing a room filled with many of those who had bullied me for years. I didn't care. I was ready. I was more than ready.

I took a deep breath and began. What followed was a solid, passionate, probably loud and definitely overly dramatic audition. It was also flawless.

I relentlessly badgered my Drama teacher. I was adamant about being in the play. I refused to be pushed aside. And it worked. I got the part and I did the work. I memorized my lines.

I paid attention during rehearsals. And I became someone different. I was no longer the weird, twitchy object of derision, I was an ACTOR.

On stage, it was as if I was the character. Every line, every movement, every moment was natural and effortless. I was Fabian. Not only that, but I was given a song to sing, that was usually done by another character.

Sadly, for him, our Feste was hopelessly tone deaf. I, most fortunately, am not. So, the closing song was mine. I will never forget walking out to the center of that darkened stage and singing those amazing centuries' old words.

I clearly remember singing the last words of the song. I stopped and bowed. There wasn't a sound. You could have heard the proverbial pin drop. It seemed to go on forever. Then the audience erupted into long and enthusiastic applause. I had done it.

Did everything change after that night? Of course not. Same bullies. Same bullshit. But, I had experienced my first real success, and I was hungry for more. I also learned one of my most important lessons and was able to write one of my first rules.

Becoming Unstoppable often means doing the exact opposite of what others are telling you to do. If they tell you to sit down and shut up. What you should do, must do, is stand up and sing.

CHAPTER 4

End at the beginning

Looking back at it now, I recognize that I had a better sense of who I was, and what I was capable of doing, when I was a child, than I did on that horrible/beautiful day when I seriously considered killing myself.

I don't think that this is in any way unusual. I think that many of us, if not in fact most of us, have a greater sense of self as children than we do as adults. It makes sense, if you think about it. When you have not lived that many years, there has been less time for the world to write your rule book for you.

If you ask a little boy if he can sing, he won't answer you, he will just start singing. If you ask a little girl if she can dance, I would suggest you get out of the way, because she is going to need the floor space.

Now, if you ask those same questions of older children, the responses are quite different. No singing. No dancing. Typically, all you will get is denial and embarrassment. But why? Simple. If you have been told often enough to sit down and shut up . . . you sit down and shut up.

If you tell a child that he can't sing, or she can't dance, pretty soon it is true. If you tell children that they are not smart, or funny, or pretty, or loved, they will believe you. Why wouldn't they? You are an adult, so you know everything. If you said it, it must be true. And from that moment onward, their hopes and dreams and lives just get smaller and smaller and smaller. Until they are not really lives at all.

Certainly not the ones they could have had, had we not helped them to "know better".

In one strange and wonderful way, I was luckier than most children, because insofar as I was just that twitchy, noisy, annoying weirdo, most of the adults in my life pretty much ignored me. I wasn't subjected to a lot of the "constructive" criticism that is typically shared with children. That simple fact, allowed me to do and try and be many different things.

For example, when I was around fifteen I wanted to have more pocket money than my family could afford to give me. So, I went looking for a part time job. Now, I grew up in a fairly small town. Everybody pretty much knew everybody else, so nobody was all that interested in having me working for them. I guess that they thought I would be a nuisance, if not a downright liability.

Well, it was clear I wasn't going to be working for someone else. How about working for myself? What special skills did I have that could become a job? What did I do best? Well, truth be told, I didn't do anything all that well. I thought about it all that week and finally inspiration struck.

The next Saturday morning, I took what little money I had, plus some I borrowed from my mother, and I bought some supplies. Then, I asked my step-father if I could have one of his big old wine making buckets. I loaded all of this onto the back of my bicycle and headed down the road. I went merrily from street to street, knocking on door after door, selling myself as a car cleaner. I had never actually cleaned a car before, but how hard could it be?

Almost immediately it became apparent that, while cleaning a car was probably not going to be all that difficult, getting someone to hire me to do it was. I got a lot of no's. A lot. However, I also got the opportunity to learn what I was doing wrong.

I learned what to say and how to say it. I learned the best time to knock on the door and how hard. I also learned not to quit. Instead of giving in after the first rejection, or the twenty first, I learned to just keep going. It really wasn't all that tough. After all, I had survived the relentless abuse of the bullies at my school; what was some suburban housewife going to do that would make me give up.

Then it happened! I got my first car to wash. Then I got another one. And another. And another. Within a few weeks, I had a thriving car cleaning business. I was working at a job of my own choosing, setting my own hours, making my own rules, and earning four times as much money as I would have if I had been giving one of those part time jobs I had tried, so desperately, to get.

Even better, my clients were becoming my friends and, better still, my mentors. They didn't know my history. They didn't know my problems. They didn't know my pain. All they knew, is that I was that cheerful young bloke, who did a really good job on their cars. I was being accepted for who I was and what I could do, instead of who I wasn't and what I couldn't do. It was an amazing feeling.

Before long, I took the risk of going farther down the road, to where the big houses were, and knocking on their front doors. Soon, I was cleaning some pretty expensive cars. One of my clients had an Aston Martin DB9 – James Bond's car! – and not only would he let me wash it, he let me drive it out of the garage.

He would also stay around and talk to me. I guess that he had taken a shine to me, because he too had grown up in a house where money was hard to come by. He had made a better life for himself and saw that I was trying to do that too, so he was only too willing to share what he had learned along the way.

Over the past few years, I have been able to have gained the support, and even friendship, of many successful people. This is because, in the beginning, it was me who made the first move. I would approach these smart, capable, successful, people and I would ask them if I could talk to them. Most of them were delighted to do so. Soon, I was being approached by others. They wanted to talk to me. But why?

One of the greatest truths of life, is often called the "Law of Attraction". It simply means, that whatever energy you are putting out, is the same kind of energy you are likely to receive. Positive, powerful, creative and dynamic energy will attract the exact same energy.

The more successful I was becoming, in both life and business, the more successful people I attracted. And I was attracting them, because I had made a choice.

I could easily, given the experiences of my past, have chosen to hate my life and everything in it. I could have cursed the heavens for my affliction and blamed the world for my failures. Why not? It's easy. Maybe it could even be argued that I would be justified to feel that way. Poor little twitchy me. But, I didn't go down that road.

Instead, I chose to do the exact opposite. I chose, and continue to choose, to put myself in life's way. Each new experience, good and bad, success and failure, has added something invaluable to my knowledge and awareness. Each new person I meet gives me the unequaled opportunity to either share or to learn something of immense and immediate value. Even the smallest of things or thoughts can change the world. At the very least, it can change yours.

I do not know what your beliefs on this subject might be, but mine are pretty clear. I do not believe that the Universe takes sides. I also do not believe that it is in the business of keeping score. Instead, I chose to believe that we are constantly being given the opportunity to grow and change for the better.

You are also given great gifts, in almost equal measure to the challenges you will face. One of the many lessons I have learned through the kindness and generosity of my many mentors: is that once you commit to doing something out of your ordinary, extraordinary things will happen.

Johann Wolfgang von Goethe, the eighteenth century writer and philosopher, once said:

"Until one is committed, there is hesitancy, the chance to draw back. Concerning all acts of initiative and creation, there is one elementary truth that, the ignorance of which, kills countless ideas and splendid plans: that the moment one definitely commits oneself, then Providence moves too. All sorts of things occur to help one that would never otherwise have occurred. A whole stream of events issues from the decision, raising in one's favor all manner of unforeseen incidents and meetings and material assistance, which no man could have dreamed would have come his way. Whatever you can do, or dream you can do, begin it. Boldness has genius, power, and magic in it. Begin it now."

In other words, once you get up off your backside and try something new, no matter what else happens, you are guaranteed a new learning opportunity, a new life changing experience, and the chance to write a new rule. Even if it is not to ever do that particular thing again.

Over the years, I have come to expect that I can count on many surprising and wonderful "coincidences" presenting themselves to me. Often in the most unexpected ways. Even past failures, have shown themselves to have been amazing opportunities.

Louis L'Amour, another writer of great insight, once said: "Adventure is often only disaster viewed in retrospect." We must never lose sight, that our past failures are the foundation of our current – and future – success.

He also wrote: "There will come a time when you believe everything is finished; that will be the beginning." It certainly was for me. That terrible/beautiful day when my life changed for good, in all the meanings of that word, has allowed me to focus on the positive aspects off my life, learn invaluable lessons from those that were negative, and use all of these experiences to continue to write the rules of my life.

Ironically, I now view myself as quite fortunate to have lived all these tears with Tourettes. What began as my enemy, has strangely become my friend. Obviously, I didn't always feel this way, but I have come to realize that I have learned more invaluable life lessons from this, than I could have ever learned had I not been so afflicted.

I was forced, from a very early age, to learn to somehow safely negotiate a veritable mine field of apparently "no-win" situations.

As a result, the adult me is far better equipped than the average person to overcome many of the experiences that this same "average" person would find devastating. My school yard history of having the snot, crap, and self-esteem kicked out of me on a daily basis, has prepared me for the many challenges that face all of us on that same daily basis. I learned that both fists and failures hurt, but you get past the pain and, no matter how much you might wish at that moment it would, humiliation doesn't kill you.

As a young man, I was convinced that, ultimately, I was going to inevitably end up broken, homeless and alone. In far too many ways, I did those things that both reinforced that conviction and contributed to the circumstances that would likely have brought it to reality. Bad choices, bad habits, bad rules, all brought me far too close to the edge.

I believe that all of us pick up our fears and insecurities along the way. We are not born with them. We are born to sing and dance. We learn to sit down and shut up. We learn to fear from our families and friends, no matter how well intentioned they may be.

I knew what I was like. I knew that I twitched and squeaked and generally annoyed or frightened everyone around me, I didn't need them to keep reminding me of it, or coming up some new and better way of being anybody but myself. I needed their support and understanding, but that was almost impossible for them to give. They didn't understand it. They didn't even know what it was, so how could they give me their support? What would that even have looked like?

In the end, I was diagnosed. I learned exactly what it was that was wrong with me. Did it change anything? Not even a little bit. Well, maybe just a little bit. But, giving something a name, does not make it miraculously go away. Okay, I knew what to call it.

However, I still did not know what to do with it. Any more than you know what to do with whatever "affliction" is holding you back from becoming who you are really meant to be. Most of you don't even have the small comfort of a diagnosis.

There is no long and incomprehensible Latin name for your problem. There is just confusion and frustration and exhaustion. I certainly know what that feels like. I also know what it feels like when that all goes away. And it feels more wonderful than you imagine.

CHAPTER 5

Happy families?

As we begin to take this journey together, I am going to invite you to stop thinking about your life and start living it. Obviously, there is some reason, or possibly many reasons, that have made you chose to read this book. And I am delighted that you have.

One of the greatest joys of my new life, is having the opportunity to share my life's lessons with others. If I can get anyone past a problem, over a stumbling block, or around an emotional pothole, I consider my life fulfilled.

My happiest day, however, will come when you finally realize that you no longer need this book and hand it along to a family member or dear friend who is struggling to find their true path.

Before then, until then, I will be here for you. I will encourage you to forget about needing to be perfect, and I will support you as you stop worrying about how others are going to react, or worse yet, what they might think about you. Let it go.

I have learned that there are just as many people out there who want you to succeed, as there are those who want you to fail. Actually, there are more. Even people who do not even know you, want you to be successful. Because, then maybe, just maybe, they could become successful too.

I have also learned to recognize – and release – those people around me who are threatened by the success of others. The very best thing you can learn to do, to become truly unstoppable, is to simply turn around and walk away from someone, anyone, who is affecting you negatively. You don't need to be rude, even though they are, you just need to be determined.

Of course many of these people are difficult, if not downright impossible to remove from your life. Family, friends, co-workers, your boss, even your spouse, can all be that negative force in your life and while you may not be able to, or even want to, put them out of your life, you can certainly find ways to put them out of your head.

Making the heartfelt and committed decision to stop listening to their voices and start listening to your own, will reduce their impact to that of a leaky faucet. They will stop being the deciding forces in your life, and just become a bunch of little drips.

I won't try and mislead you here. You will lose some of these people. They will not be able to relate to the new you, or to the new dynamic of your relationship with them. They will move on. And you will be grateful for their leaving.

Invariably, inevitably, someone way cooler will come along and fill up the space they left. Just as nature abhors a vacuum, so too does the Universe.

Whenever someone who is holding you back leaves your physical or emotional world, someone new will come along to take their place. What you need to do, is make sure that you are in the position to attract the right kind of people. What kind of people?

The kind of people who can help you, and support you, and guide you, and push you, and celebrate you, as you become the REAL you. The YOU you were always meant to be.

In my work, I meet so many people who are trapped by the fears and the doubts and the restrictions that have been imposed on them by others. By people we know and trust. Most of these fears, doubts and restrictions are, in fact, caused by the very people who are supposed to love us without measure. Our family. Mothers, fathers, brothers, sisters, or, in my case, my Grandmother.

Viewed by most people as the quintessential image of the kindly old Granny, she was actually the Nazi death camp guard of my young life. She hated everything about me. The way I twitched. The sounds I made. I swear, she hated the very sight of me. How could something like me, have ever come from her family?

Around others, she would simply turn away. She would hide her embarrassment and disgust away from their eyes. Alone, however, it was a very different story. I won't go into detail as to how she used to treat me and what she used to say and do, but believe me when I tell you it was horrible.

It would have been devastating to anyone, but to someone already on his way down the long and slippery road to black depression and crippling anxiety, it was nothing short of torture. I could not tell anyone about this, certainly not my parents, because I had no reason to believe that anyone would believe me. There was my "Nan-nan", saintly old woman that she appeared to be, and here I was, all twitchy and weird. Who would you have voted off the island?

Now, I must take this opportunity to tell you that my parents never abused me in any physical way. My mother was my angel. True, she didn't understand me, or at least what was happening to me, but she loved me without hesitation or limit. Both my father and, later, my stepfather were decent men. They had their own issues sure, but I was not one of them. They always treated me with kindness and, in the case of my father, a certain benign neglect. No, my problem was my "Nan-nan".

My parents would send me to her house for at least two weeks every year. Every year, I would become more and more anxious and afraid, as the time for my "holiday" would approach. No matter what reason I could give, or excuse I could think of, I could never get out of going. By the time I got there, I would be a nervous twitchy wreck. And soon, the cycle of abuse would begin.

It always started off innocently. She would interrupt something I was doing. Usually, it was a chore I had been given.

In time I would come to understand that she delighted in setting me up to fail, but, back then, all I knew is that I could never please her. Whatever it was I was supposed to be doing, I was doing it wrong. She took absolute delight in criticizing and belittling me. That is how it would always begin.

Next, she would start comparing me to my father – whom she hated – and it would go on from there. Why she hated him, never really became clear to me, but hate him she did. And I was just like him. This was her favorite rant. He was awful, I was worse, and neither of us was worthy of being in her family.

I heard this so often from her, I could have repeated it word for word along with her, like some kind of psychotic Greek Chorus.

I learned, through painstaking and physically painful tutelage, a few basic things from her. First, I was no good. Just basically a waste of life and air. Second, I wasn't going to ever amount to anything. Next, I was just like my father and she hated me every bit as much as she hated him. And finally, I was never going to amount to anything, certainly not like her other grandchildren. You know, the ones she loved.

She would keep going at this, becoming louder and more hysterical as each moment passed, until finally she would snap. At this point, it became physical. She would slap me, and punch me, and push and pull me around the room. If I tried to defend myself, it would become worse.

Eventually, she would haul me stumbling down the hallway and throw me into the tiny, dingy room in which I slept and I would be forced to remain there until this particular storm had passed.

If this had happened only once, it would have been a damaging experience and scarring memory for a child as young as I was, but this was to become the norm. It was a scenario that would play out for years. Never different. Never better.

The worst part about it was . . . I believed her. I must be deserving of this kind of treatment. The logic is not hard to understand. She was my mother's mother. I loved my mother. My mother loved her. She trusted her. She sent me there to stay with her. Maybe this is what she wanted me to learn. So I did.

A recent United Nations survey has revealed that an average of six out of ten children, between the ages of two and fourteen, are routinely mentally or physically abused. Often it is both.

This study included accounts from almost 200 countries. It is not, in any way imaginable, an isolated problem. I recently attended a conference that focused on the issue of living with disabilities. I was the keynote speaker for a group of over 900 individuals, many of whom were themselves living with a physical or mental disability.

Whenever possible, at one of these events, I like to arrive a little early and silently slip into one or two of the other sessions. It gives me the opportunity to get a quick read on the nature and energy of the group involved. This time, I was in for one of the biggest surprises of my life.

I quietly entered the room and joined a session in progress. It was about the nature of disability and its effect on self-esteem. At one point, the presenter asked the group for a show of hands. "How many of you", he asked, "have ever been mentally, physically, and/or sexually abused by others?" I was shocked to see almost sixty percent of the audience raise their hands.

Most families carry a shameful past, where acts of abuse are both cruelly common and quietly hidden away. It becomes a conspiracy of denial and delusion. Every group therapy session I have ever attended, is filled with these lost souls. Emotionally confused and spiritually broken by the reality of their upbringing, as compared to the idyllic childhoods we are taught by popular fiction to believe that everyone else is enjoying.

Such denial has been proven time and time again, to carry a kind "echo" effect. A child is abused. The child grows into an adult. The adult becomes an abuser. And so on. And so on. The circle will be unbroken. At least until somebody, anybody, does something to break it. Easy to say, almost impossible to do.

This is because we, those of us who have been abused, are also oddly willing participants in this conspiracy of silence and denial. We have become the guardians of all of the dirty little secrets from our past. We have become keepers of the shadows, instead of keepers of the flame. And I am as guilty as anyone.

I cannot fully express how difficult it was for me to open up the dark and scary corners of my memory and truly look at my history in the cold light of day. I did it, because if you intend to live the unstoppable life for which you yearn, you must first actively release yourself from the past. Your past.

I can show you how to do this, in the only way I know how, by inviting you to join me in the painful examination of my own. I promise you that I will be honest, in both the events that took place, and the emotional damage they caused. This is not going to be easy, for either of us, but stick with me.

What I am about to tell you, may be as personal for you, as it is for me. My experiences are, by no means, unusual. You may have known someone to whom this has happened. It may have happened in your own family. This story may help you to better understand, and learn to overcome, your own demons. At the very least, it will help you to better understand mine and how they brought me to where I am. And, above all, remember, it is by overcoming the demons of your past, that you can become the hero of your future.

Perhaps I was lucky. One day my dear old Nan-Nan slipped up. Without any provocation, she began to smack me about. Only, this time, she did so in front of my Mother. I remember screaming at her, that now she could not deny what was happening to me. I had not been lying. This is what I had been suffering the whole time. For the rest of that day, I refused to come out of my room, even for meals. The next morning we left and I never went back. Well, actually, I did but that is a story I will tell you later.

CHAPTER 6

The sins of the father

On paper, we were the quintessential suburban family. Oh sure, the kid was a little weird, but the parents were perfect. Mother was a well-respected and much beloved teacher. Even better, Father was a highly accomplished medical professional.

Each day, they would go off to their respective offices and bask in the admiration of the community. Intelligent, charming, successful, they were the envy of the town, or at least our neighborhood. "They seem so happy", the neighbors would say. They could not have been more wrong.

I have learned, much later in life, that most families carry some kind of shameful secret. Mine certainly did. The bizarre part of this is, at the time, nobody thinks it is anything but normal. I certainly didn't.

In spite of what the neighbors might have thought, all was not perfect in our house. It wasn't even close. Because of their busy professional lives, my parents could easily avoid one another for most of the day.

Mornings were a blur of getting washed, dressed and ready for the day. Hurriedly bolting down a few bites of breakfast and racing out the door, successfully avoiding any but the briefest of interactions. Off we would go, to his office for my Father. To her classroom for my Mother. To another journey through the depths of Hell for me.

Although we almost always left the house together in the morning, we all came back to it separately. Often I would be the first to arrive. I can clearly remember those few brief moments of quiet.

The blissful calm before the emotional storm that I knew was coming. It is truly amazing to me, what we can so easily accept as normal. This was ours.

On most weekdays, my Mother would arrive home shortly after I did. She was a lovely woman. Kind, gentle, quick to laugh. But, there was always a slight tension. She would almost "hum", like a violin string wound too tight. Her way of dealing with this tension, was a glass of sherry. Actually, it was usually four or five glasses.

I can still picture her sitting in her favorite chair, mindlessly watching something on television, and getting up every five minutes or so to pour herself another glass. What I did not know at the time, was that she was preparing herself for the inevitable events that would follow. I just thought she was thirsty.

My Father would arrive a little later and, at first, it would seem reasonably pleasant. It is interesting how easy it is to avoid each other, even in a relatively small space. Mother would be in the kitchen, making dinner. Father in the living room, watching television. Me somewhere, doing something, but eventually we would have to come together and that is when it would come apart.

Inevitably, within minutes of starting the meal, the bitterness and resentments each of them harbored toward the other would begin to show. It was like watching some never ending emotional tennis match. Serve and volley. Smash. Return. Rush the net. Just like tennis, there were lots of faults. And, just like tennis, "love" meant nothing.

For years, I was their audience. The silent witness to their anger and frustration. To their misery and regret. To their sadness and hostility. The only problem was, I just thought it was dinner.

Seriously, I did not think that this was wrong. I did not even think that it was unusual. I thought that we were a perfectly normal family and that what was happening at our dinner table, was happening at dinner tables all throughout our town. Obviously, there must have been other homes in which this was happening. Maybe it even happened in yours. Maybe it still is.

All I knew, is that the pattern would play itself out, virtually unchanged, each evening. The conversation would become an argument. The argument would become a fight. The dinner table would become a battlefield. And the combatants, no matter how badly wounded, would keep relentlessly moving through the trenches, sniping at each other.

Until the sound of broken dishes would signal the start of this evening's cease fire. An uneasy truce would be formed and the battle weary survivors would stumble off in search of some small space in which to nurse their wounds. My mother would retreat to the kitchen or bedroom, to quietly cry. My Father would retreat to the living room, to sit staring blankly at the television. I would simply pick up the pieces of shattered china and try to be as quiet as I could.

Obviously, I was not completely oblivious to how unhappy they were. I certainly knew my Mother was. The crying was a pretty good clue. What I did not realize, is how miserable my Father was. He was one of those men who never let anyone in. Aside from the anger he would show toward my Mother, he kept everything else to himself.

His emotions were trapped away, somewhere deep within. I didn't know it at the time, but I was learning one of the worst lessons of my life from him. Simply through casual, yet endlessly repeated, observation. He was my role model. He was my teacher. And I have always been a good student.

It would have been quite easy to assume that my Father was living an Unstoppable Life. He was a well-educated professional. He was a highly respected Dentist, in a family practice with my Mother's brother. He was a man of stature and status in our community. And he was a hopeless drug addict.

Just as my Mother would find a little solace in her sherry bottle, my Father had his own avenue of escape. His was Valium, the drug of choice for much of the Swinging Sixties. Like a busy little squirrel, he would stash the tiny brown bottles away, as if in preparation for the coming winter. They were immediately available to him at home, at the office, even in his car.

He was never more than a few feet away from his secret supply. I eventually learned that my Uncle was also addicted to Valium and the two of them would merrily write each other fresh prescriptions whenever they started to run short. Toward the end of his addiction, my Father would be eating pills like candy.

I can see know, just how miserably unhappy and deeply depressed he was. Because he had the – questionable – luxury of being able to endlessly prescribe his preferred method of avoiding facing up to the reality of his life, he didn't. He would simply sit there, in a cloud of cigarette smoke, and lose himself in the mindless haze of prescription drugs and late night television.

Whenever I would try to talk to him, his responses seemed to come, if they came at all, from the bottom of a very deep well. I did not truly understand what was happening and, even if I had, there was nothing I could have done to change the situation.

The only thing I could do, was become like him. I had already learned, thanks to the bullies at school and my "happy holidays" with my Grandmother, how to keep my emotions hidden. What I now had learned from my Father, was how to mitigate the pain. Some fathers and sons share jokes and hobbies, we shared Valium and denial.

The situation at home remained the same for a very long time, but a change was coming. Unfortunately, it was not destined to be a change for the better. Like the old joke says, "I used to say that things could be worse, and sure enough they got worse."

After years of living in a desperately unhappy marriage, my parents decided that something had to change. Like most couples in a situation like this, they had choices. Counselling was one option. Divorce was another. My parents, however, were a little more creative. They chose to become involved in one of the more interesting social experiments of the Sixties. Wife swapping.

For the record, it was my Father who was the instigator in this next chapter of our family's little melodrama. My Mother went along with it, because . . . well, anything must be better than what they had. And so it was, that, for the next three years, I lived in a real life version of "Bob & Carol & Ted & Alice". (Look it up on IMDB) It was as if I had two sets of parents. It was perfectly natural, dare I say normal, for me to wake up Saturday morning and find my Father in bed with my "other mother" and my Mother in another bed with my "other father".

I know that some of you must be shocked and appalled, but I actually have quite fond memories of those days. These were the only times I remember my parents being – almost – happy. There was no screaming and crying and dishes being thrown. I finally saw my parents laughing and enjoying themselves. The fact that they were also in the arms of someone else, could not have mattered less to me. It seemed as if the war was over. Peace had reigned supreme. For a time.

It didn't last, of course. When something, anything, is only the sublimation of a feeling, the time comes when it is no longer enough. The drugs and alcohol had not worked and, so too, the polyamorous lifestyle they had adopted was destined to fail. It was my Mother who cracked first. The weekends she was spending in the arms of another man, were not enough to make up for the rest of the time she had to spend with my Father. The fights were getting worse, with the worst one soon to come.

The final one was my fault. I had stubbornly refused to go to bed. Maybe I thought that, if they could do whatever they wanted, so could I. I was wrong, and my Father was most explicit in his remarks as to that fact. I do not remember ever seeing him that angry. Instantly, my Mother came to my defense.

All this did, was turn the full force of his anger onto her. I will never forget the look in my Father's eyes. If looks could really kill, I would have lost my Mother that night. Instead, it was the night she found herself. Her own eyes filled with tears, she stood up to him. For herself. For me.

He moved toward her. I don't know what he had intended to do. I didn't bother to wait to find out.

Grabbing my Mother's silver scissors from her sewing table, I forced my way between them. I thrust the tiny scissors at my Father, like the sharpest of swords, and screamed: "Leave my mother alone. I hate you . . . leave my mother alone."

I don't remember much else about that night, or the days that followed, but I do know that my Mother had decided to leave. When the time came, my Father tried to stop us. He came rushing out of the house; begging us to stay. Things would be different. Things would be better. But, it was all too little. And much too late.

I can still remember that morning, as clearly as if were just yesterday. My Father was hanging onto the door of the car, begging for another chance. My Mother was crying and shaking her head . . . no. I could see the panic in her eyes.

I was terrified, not by my Father's shouting, but by the very possibility that she would weaken and change her mind. There was no way that I could ever face going back into that house. Back into that sad and miserable life.

Grabbing my Mother's hand, I leaned across the car and screamed into my Father's face.

"You had your chance . . . we are leaving . . . and we are never coming back."

Stunned, he stepped back and we drove away. I kept hold of her hand and repeated over and over again, "Keep driving, Mother . . . don't stop . . . just keep driving."

As we travelled farther and farther away from the only home I had never known, I was not filled with sadness.

No, it was as if a great weight was being lifted off my chest. I could breathe. Fully and finally, I could breathe. I did not know where we were going, but I knew that it would have to be better than from where we had come. And it was.

My Mother married a wonderful man. They have now been together for over forty years. After all this time, they still hold hands. Bickering one minute, laughing the next. I love them both beyond limit. In my early twenties, I decided that this dear man was more a father to me than my own. This explains the hyphen.

I am "Ellis" by my birth, but "Myers" by my heart. This man is my true father and I will be devastated when he is gone. Until then, I will continue to show them my love and my gratitude. For they have taught me the meaning of both.

CHAPTER 7

And now for something completely different

If you think that the previous chapter was hard to read, just imagine how hard it was to write.

Memories, especially long suppressed ones, are difficult for anyone. Everyone today knows a little something about PTSD – Post Traumatic Stress Disorder – but, unless you experience it yourself, you cannot truly comprehend its horrors. It is even worse for someone already suffering from a variety of emotional and psychological problems.

Each memory that gets dredged up from the bottom of our psyche, becomes a gateway into the very same emotions we felt on that day. It is as if we are reliving the experience. I am doing this for two reasons.

One, it was long overdue for me to acknowledge and accept the complex mix of symptoms and circumstances that brought me to that terrible/beautiful day, on which I was reunited with myself. And, two, I am hoping that, by my being painfully honest with you, you might take the chance to be honest about your own pain. Anyway, the story continues.

By the time I reached my teens, an already awkward time for almost all of us, I was a completely confused and totally twitchy nightmare on feet. My Tourettes was full blown and impossible to hide.

At that particular time in the development of my condition, I had a rather unique twitch that would always seem to manifest itself at the most inopportune moments possible. When the anxiety would build up to the point that I could no longer control it, it would begin.

At first, rather innocuously, I would begin to blow on my hand. Then I would point at some imaginary thing or person in front of me, while looking repeatedly under any table that happened to be nearby. At the same time, I would be squeaking and making small chirping sounds. In addition, I would be squinting my eyes, shaking my head, and hopping up and down. This would continue for as long as it took for the obsessive/compulsive need to go away.

Needless to say, I was not all that attractive to the pretty girls in my class. It is not that I went entirely unnoticed, of course. I got plenty of attention. It just wasn't the kind of attention any child needs.

Like most children who suffer at the hands of bullies, I thought it was my own fault. I was obviously doing something to cause this abuse. My condition was not the problem, I was.

Frankly, at that time, I still didn't know that what was wrong with me had a name. I didn't know that I had Tourettes, I just thought I was a freak. And I had a lot of people around me who were more than happy to agree with me.

I was also very reluctant to tell my parents about what was happening to me at school, in the misguided fear that it would somehow affect their opinion of me and they would realize that they should start treating me in the same way as did the bullies at school. Crazy doesn't have to make sense.

And I was a little crazy. Not because I had a mental condition; I was actually not that bothered by my rather large compendium of ticks and twitches; but because of the stress and anxiety caused by the relentless bullying.

Today, this kind of abuse is looked upon as a real problem, with horrifying results. Teen drug addiction, alcoholism, and suicides – both attempted and successful – are all now being attributed to bullying. Back then, however, it was just "kids being kids".

As only one of countless survivors of bullying, I have no tolerance for it, and no clear understanding of why it is even remotely tolerated. I live in hope that, one day, it will be no more socially acceptable than child sexual abuse. A bully is nothing more than a pederast with his pants on. A bully robs his – or her – victim of all self-respect. Of all pride and confidence. Of any positive sense of worth and value.

It is a well understood truism, that bullies are cowards. They try and overcome the fear inside them, by making others fear them. All of that is well and good, when viewed from the relative safety of the future. At the moment it is happening to you, the only thing that matters is your own pain.

I assure you that I never gave a moment's thought as to why they were abusing me. I just knew that they were. And I wanted, more than anything, for someone – anyone – to make them stop.

Sadly, I knew that nobody would. Not my teachers, not the school administration, not the other kids, not even my parents. There was no cavalry charging over the hill to my rescue. I would have to do it myself. I began to realize that it is not the actual bullying that does the damage, it is the way we take that bullying to heart.

It is in how we, the victims, choose to perceive what is happening to us and, through that distorted perspective, begin to justify these actions.

It is true; we start to believe; I am ugly. I am stupid. I am different. I am weird, or fat, or just plain wrong. In my case, it was easy. All anybody had to do was spend five minutes with me and they could see. I was very, very different. Was I responsible for the way in which these people were treating me? No. But I was very much responsible for what it was doing to me. I was becoming a partner in my own abuse. I was becoming one of them. How was I doing this?

Simple. I believed them. I allowed them to convince me that I was every terrible thing they said about and to me.

It took me a long time to understand this. It took me even longer to change it. Their voices were in my head for years. To this day, I can still hear them off in the distance. I just choose to no longer listen. I have made the clear and conscious choice to be my own champion. I am the cavalry charging to my own rescue. Mine is the voice to which I will listen. Mine are the rules I will follow.

At this point, at least for some of you, I am sure you are thinking, "Well, if he is saying – listen to your own voice – why should I be listening to him?" Not an entirely unreasonable question. As long as you are also entirely certain, that the voice in your head, is your own.

For most of us, it simply isn't. It certainly wasn't for me. I thought it was. I was positive that I was in control. In charge of my life. In charge of my thoughts. It turns out I was wrong. How did I come to realize this?

Simple, the voice in my head kept telling me I was wrong. It would tell me I was less than I was. It would tell me that I was incapable of succeeding. That I would fail. That I would lose. That I was nothing. Certainly nothing worth anything. And for the longest time, I believed that voice.

Just as you are believing the voice in your head. The voice that is keeping you from being/trying/having everything you want. The voice that is keeping you "safe". At least, that is what the voice is telling you it is doing. Be safe. Stay safe. Play it safe. Safety first.

I lived that way, and listened to that voice, for most of my life. I couldn't help myself. I was always afraid. I was always anxious and insecure. I was always looking for that safe place where I didn't have to always be watching my back. Where I didn't have to try and become so small that nobody would notice me. Some safe place where the bullies couldn't find me. I searched for that place and I kept searching until I found it. And it was in the last place I would have ever looked.

It was on that terrible/beautiful day that I found the safe place I had been searching for, for all of those years. I found it in myself. I was standing on the ninth floor balcony of my apartment – the one in which I now lived alone – trying to figure out if the fall would actually kill me, when I experienced what I can only call an epiphany.

I realized that all of the pain and misery I carried; all of the unresolved issues of my childhood; all of the suffocating rules and restrictions that had been placed on me by others; all of the frustrations and failures I had felt because my life was not perfect; all of this mind numbing crap in my head; was the real reason I was standing out there in the wind.

I instantly recognized, that my life was not the problem, it was how I was choosing to see it, and therefore react to it, that was the problem. I was viewing my life through the dirty window of anxiety and depression. Dim and murky and distorted, it was changing the reality of any given situation into something that was destined to be dreadful.

Whether it needed to be, or, more likely, not. I suddenly realized that, all I needed to do, was to get on the right side of that window. Get out into the world, the real world, and no longer stand in the shadows behind that tear streaked window. So, how did it go?

At first, it was horrible. Dazed and confused would best describe the good days. The bad ones were something else again. It was to be expected. When most of us are confronted with any new experience requiring change, we are more likely to revert back to our old ways and run screaming from the room. When you have been living for any length of time on auto-pilot, taking the controls into your own hands is a little scary.

Actually, it is a lot scary. And then, after a while, it isn't. They say (whoever they are) that you can make or break a habit in fourteen days. It took me a little longer than that.

It was also a lot harder than I thought it was going to be, but the first thing I learned, is the first thing I am going to teach you.

GIVE YOURSELF A BREAK!

You are going to screw up at this. It isn't easy and you have no experience in doing it. There are times, like this, when you simply have to realize that true and lasting change is difficult. It is going to get messy. And not everyone is going to jump right in there to help you.

In fact, it is more likely to be the exact opposite. And it is easy to understand why. They don't want you to stop listening to their voices. That has been working out just fine for them. They don't want to stop being able to push your buttons. After all, they installed them for a reason. But, for this to work, you just have to do it. Step back. Take a deep breath. And try again. Make that new rule. And then another.

In time, it becomes automatic. You quickly recognize it when the old voices speak up. And you will just as quickly learn to quieten them with your own. You will become more and more confident in the truth of what you are hearing, when you finally begin to listen exclusively to your own voice.

Now, I am not suggesting that you should never seek out, and even accept, the opinions of others. Lots of other people have great and wonderful insights that you can learn by, and brilliant and effective solutions that you can use. It is, however, up to you to make the critical determination of what is going to be right for you. For you.

I know that you likely have families. Wives, husbands, children, parents. You also have friends and co-workers, bosses and people who rely on you. So, you are responsible to and for these people. How does this fit in with what I am saying about listening to your own voice?

It is kind of like the part in the inflight safety demonstration when they talk about the safety mask. Always remember, you have to put your own mask on first . . . before you can be of any help to others.

This is critically important. Pay attention. I am serious about what I am about to say. We are not here in this world, here in this life, just for ourselves. We are here for each other. Some more. Some less. But here, together, we are.

And we have to learn to be of help to one another. Once our masks are on, we have to be both willing and able to help other people with theirs. It is the only reason we are here. And the only way this world can hope to keep working. It sounds like a contradiction, doesn't it? Put yourself first, but help others. It took me a long time to find the balance. It is, in fact, the primary reason I now do what I do. But it was not easy. Not at all.

There was a time when all of this seemed impossible to me. The vital, successful, impactful life I lead now, was not only improbable back then, it was unthinkable. I HAVE TOURETTES! Are you kidding me? I am going to be a public speaker. I can barely get people to listen to me in private and I am going to somehow get people to pay me to talk to them. Yeah. That is going to happen. And yet, it did. And still, it does.

The first time I ever stepped onto a stage, not as a character in a play – that I knew I could do – but as myself, good old twitchy me, I thought I was going to crap my pants. The voice in my head, my own voice, was screaming at me, "One twitch, one squeak, and you are done, Buddy. This game will be over and you will be finished." As they were making my introduction, I was seriously thinking, "I should run." I walked out there like a condemned man heading to his execution. I started to look around for the door. I was pretty sure I could make it.

Then something happened. I started to look at the faces in the audience. The ones nearest the door first, of course. Then the others. I slowly began to realize that they were interested in me. In what I might have to say. In the ways in which I might be able to help them. Teach them. Show them something that could make their jobs, their lives, a little easier, a little better, or, at the very least, a little different. I don't even remember what I said. I only remember the faces.

If I had listened to my fears. If I had listened to the admonition to run for the door. If I had reverted to my old self, I would not be here today. I don't mean that I wouldn't have this job. I mean I probably would have ultimately found myself on another balcony. There is no way I would have ever learned what an Unstoppable Life even looked like, let alone the glorious reality of living one.

CHAPTER 8

You can get there from here

Recently, I spoke at a conference for over 400 municipal clerks and treasurers. It was held at Blue Mountain, Ontario, a stunningly beautiful ski resort just north of Toronto. After humbly accepting their generous standing ovation, I made my way back to the nearest airport.

The following day, after having spent most of the night on an airplane, I presented the keynote speech for 1200 travel professionals, at Vacation.com's International Conference. This event took place at the Dolphin Hotel, located in Disneyworld.

Later that same day, I boarded another airplane for a flight to Edmonton, Alberta. I was on my way to give two presentations at "Vitalize", a national conference that celebrates the selfless work of over 800 incredible volunteers.

I hope that you do not think that I am just bragging here. I simply wanted to give you some idea of the life I have created for myself. Now, I have always had good jobs. I always worked hard. I always tried to learn the best way to do any job. I always kept my appointments, hit my goals, made my quotas. But, in spite of all that, I never felt successful.

It wasn't until I began to follow my own voice, my own rules, that I was able to begin to create the life I now live. I went from being that terrified, twitchy teenager, to being a successful public speaker with over 800 clients, including some of the largest and most well-known companies in the world. And I did it alone. I had to. And so do you.

I am not saying that nobody helped. Oh course, I had help. Some people have been remarkably helpful over the years and I will always be grateful for their guidance and their support. What I am saying, is that nobody can change your life for you. You have to do it yourself.

Why? Because you are the only one who knows where you are going. Sure, others can support you in your journey. You can listen to their advice. Gain from their experience. Take confidence from the living examples they have become, through their success and their humanity. What you cannot, must not, do, is allow them to force you into their vision of what your life should be. This kind of influence, however well intentioned, is as bad – if not worse – than the negative voices that will tell you to not even try.

Now, you might have noticed that I just said that, "you know where you are going". I am sure at least some of you went, "What?" I am also sure that you are thinking, "I have no idea where I am going." The truth of the matter is, you actually do. You just don't know you do.

When I first started to think about what I wanted to do with my life. How I wanted to live. How I wanted to be Unstoppable. I had no idea of what that looked like. I didn't know what it was, let alone how to achieve it. I just knew that my old life hadn't worked out so well for me and, if I had any chance for survival, I would have to create a new one. One that was MINE. Not one that was tortured together out of the bits and pieces of those broken dreams and broken dinner plates of my past.

The first thing I had to do was to be honest with myself. Honest about myself. Honest about others. I had to take a harsh, critical look at who I was and what I had become. I needed to know where I was, before I could begin to figure out where I was going to go.

It was not easy. Those were painful days and nights. It is not fun, and it is not pretty, to strip away all of the fantasies and fictions that we have allowed to be created around us. Yes, I said "allowed". You cannot deny that you had a part to play in how your life has turned out. You were the willing, albeit unwitting, worker in the construction of the life you have. You can, however, also be the architect of the life you want.

Socrates was the first to have said it, but wise and thoughtful souls through history have agreed:

"An unexamined life is not worth living."

This simply means that you have to stop and take a good, hard look at your life. What it is. What it isn't. And then you have to decide what you want it to be. How YOU want it to be. Not how other people want your life to be. It was listening to them, in the first place, that got you into this. So, how do you do this? Where do you start? Well, as Julie Andrews sang, in the Sound of Music, "You start at the very beginning."

I am sure that most of you are somewhat familiar with Maslow's Hierarchy of Needs. Okay, maybe not. Let me give you the condensed version of it.

First, you need to take care of your physical requirements. Food, water, sleep, etc.

Second, you need safety. A place to live and a job to pay for it.

Third, you need love. Friends, family, that someone special.

This is where most people stop. They think that this is enough. A home and a family, a job and some friends, what more could you want? Right? Wrong. There is more yet to come.

Four, you need esteem. The respect and admiration of others and, most of all, yourself.

Five, and finally, you need self-actualization. This is the big one. And this is the whole point of this book. But what is it?

One definition of self-actualization is:

"The motive to realize one's full potential; expressing one's creativity; and the quest for spiritual enlightenment, the pursuit of knowledge, and the desire to give to society."

Let's break that down into small, easy to chew, bites.

"The motive to realize one's full potential." Or, as the US Army ads used to say, "Be all you can be." This means that you need to find a way to fully use all of your own unique talents and abilities, in as frequent, and as deliberate, a way as you can.

Deep down inside, you know what you are good at doing. It might be buried under a big pile of "you can't" and "you shouldn't" and "What would people think?" but it is in there. Dig around, you'll find it. Just keep looking.

This brings us to, "expressing your creativity." That does not mean singing, or dancing, or painting, or writing free form verse. It can, but it can also mean anything that comes from your own imagination. You could think of a faster, better, cheaper, safer, more ecologically sound way of doing something, anything. Build a better mouse-trap. Or a better mouse.

Now comes a tough one. "The quest for spiritual enlightenment." This does not necessarily have a religious connotation. It can, if that is what holds meaning for you, but it does not have to. It can also be as simple as striving to achieve a true understanding of your own spirit.

I say that this is "tough", because it is one of the areas wherein there has been so much negative reinforcement throughout history. Everybody seems to want to write their own definition of what it means and force others to, not only accept it, but live by it. All I am going to say on the subject is that, no matter what you choose to believe in, make sure that it is really what YOU believe. Listen to your own voice.

Now comes one of my favorites. "The pursuit of knowledge." I cannot imagine having a day go by, wherein I have not learned something. About myself. About another. About the world in which we live. Learning is life. Life is learning.

It doesn't have to be anything huge. It doesn't have to anything life changing. It just needs to be something you didn't know before. If you can't identify something you learned today, your day isn't done. Get on with it!

And, finally, "the desire to give to society." Isn't this really what this is all about? Life. Living. It is certainly what this book is about. However grandiose and self-indulgent some people may think it is for me to have written this. For me to think that anything I might have to say, will help anybody else. To assume that I have answers, to all, to any of the questions you have about your life and how to make it better, to make it unstoppable. I only know, that this is what I can do. What I can give.

Originally, I thought I was writing it for myself, but I learned very quickly that it was not. I wrote this book for you. And the only one who can truly judge its worth, is you.

When I began writing this, I had it in mind to create a document that could better help people to understand the complexity of living with Tourettes. Very quickly, it became clear to me that many of the issues that arise around living with Tourettes, also exist in the everyday lives of most people. They just don't have a clinical diagnosis to fall back on, as an excuse for not living the life of their true choosing.

All of us are being held back in some way. Misunderstood. Misguided. Misled. By our families. By our friends. By society in general. Most of all, by ourselves. It is as if we have a 400 pound weight strapped to our back and we have to stumble around each day, just trying not to fall down. Because, we know that if we do, we will be crushed by it, and we will never be able to get up again.

That is how I felt for every day of my old life. I know the feeling of being constantly overwhelmed by life. Or at least what I thought life was. That is what finally brought me out onto that balcony. I was done. Enough was enough. In fact, it was more than enough. It was too much.

I am so very grateful for that moment of surrender. Had I not reached my breaking point, I would never have been able to face what my life had become. I would have continued to think that I could simply "fake it till I make it". Now, I must confess that I am a "hard learner". It took me a long time, and a lot of pain, until I was ready to listen to myself. I truly hope that you are not quite as stubborn as me.

I hope that you are open to the story I am sharing with you and the lessons I have learned. I hope that you are ready to become Unstoppable.

Sadly, not everyone is. Every time I spoke in front of a group of people, a few of them would come up to me and ask me questions that related to the challenges they were facing in their lives. At first, I would spend lots of time with them. Hours. I don't do that anymore.

What I learned, very quickly, is that a lot of people just like to talk about their problems. They love a shoulder to cry on. A sympathetic ear. They are simply looking for the company, that misery so dearly loves. So, I would talk to them.

Try and be honest and forthright and giving. To share and suggest and support and encourage. And then I would watch them walk away, secure in the knowledge that they would probably do absolutely nothing. How did I know this?

It is a matter of simple statistics. I learned this entirely by accident. One day, I did not have enough time to talk. I was rushing to make a flight. So, I gave them my telephone number and told them to call me in a couple of days. I would gladly talk to them then. Nobody called.

At first, I thought that maybe I had seemed rude by not taking the time to talk to them right there. Maybe they were all hurt, or insulted, because I had rushed away. So, I tried it again. With similar results. Now I give them the number and suggest a time for them to call within the next three days. Only about 1 in 100 ever calls. Statistics.

The problem with advice, even good advice, is that it is coming from outside of you. It comes to you and you have to make an instantaneous choice. To accept it. To reject it. To file it away and think about it later. It all happens in a split second. I have actually watched it happen, right in front of me.

Someone would come up to me and ask if we could talk. In many cases, it was quite easy to get to the issues that were holding them back. The root of the problem. I would begin to offer a few suggestions for dealing with the issues and overcoming the problems. And I could actually see them start to mentally filter the advice and information, through their existing set of habits and beliefs. "I could never do that." "That won't work." "What will people think of me, if I did something like that?"

In part, this is perfectly natural. We all filter any new information through our acquired knowledge and experience. Sometimes it fits, sometimes it doesn't. The problem with this, is very simple to understand. If your life isn't working, whatever that might mean to you, it is directly because of your acquired knowledge and experience.

Whenever you try to introduce a new thought, or concept, or rule, your mind immediately does a very rapid balance equation. Does this new idea, or concept, or rule fit into what I already know and believe? If it doesn't, it will be rejected.

This is called: Selective Perception. The formal definition of which is: The process by which individuals perceive what they want to, in media messages, while ignoring opposing viewpoints. It is a broad term to identify the behavior to tend to "see things" based on their own particular frame of reference.

It also describes how we categorize and interpret sensory information in a way that favors one category or interpretation over another. In other words selective perception is a form of bias, because we interpret information in a way that is congruent with our existing values and beliefs.

That is a mouthful, isn't it? Let me simplify it for you. You only hear what you want to hear. Or, to be more specific, you only hear what the voices in your head will let you hear. If it does not agree with them, they will shout it down. Each and every time.

This is called: Perceptual Defense. The voices in your head do not want you to hear conflicting information and they will do everything in their considerable power to stop it from happening. It is as if they have put their sticky fingers in your ears and are going, "la, la, la, la, la". Keep it up. Keep trying to listen to any more of this new, and to them frightening, information and they will shirt into another gear. This one is called: Perceptual Vigilance. This one is really scary. And it can ruin your life.

Perceptual vigilance is the habit by which you seek to avoid encountering any information that threatens the information you already possess. In other words, "Don't confuse me with the facts, I know what I believe." And isn't that exactly what got you here in the first place?

Look, I get it. Life is hard. Change is harder. All of us are just trying to get by. But, is getting by enough? Maybe it is. For some. It finally wasn't for me. And I am sure that it isn't for you. In fact, I know it. How do I know it? Well, you are this far into the book. That didn't happen by accident. You made a choice. Didn't you?

So, let's be realistic here. Life will knock you down. It has before. It probably is right now. It most definitely will in the future. That's life. Anyone who thinks that they can escape this, is very wrong. You just have to accept that both time and probability are working constantly against you.

Almost everything is beyond our control. Except for one very important thing. While we cannot control what happens to us, we can control how we let it affect us. We can break, or we can bend. We can fail, or we can flourish. We can give up, or we can get up.

It is what we learn through today's adversities that enables us to overcome tomorrow's. Remember what I said earlier: "Tomorrow's successes are built on the foundation of yesterday's failures."

Look at me. One day I was a perfectly normal, perfectly happy little boy. The next day I wasn't. Each new twitch took me farther and farther away from that little boy. Until he barely existed. The same thing has happened to you. Maybe not as dramatic. Likely not as visible. But, happen to you, it most definitely has. It can, however, change. It did for me. It can for you. And I will show you how.

CHAPTER 9

You think you've got it bad

I do not know what problems you are living with. What it is in your life that is stopping you from being Unstoppable. All I know, is that there is "something". Just about everybody has something that is holding them back from success, or from happiness, or simply from peace of mind. And most of them never figure out what it is.

For me, it was simple. I have a clinical diagnosis. I have Tourettes Syndrome. I know that. At least, I know that now. For a very long time I did not know what was wrong. I knew something was "wrong" with me. Everybody knew something was wrong with me. They could see it. We just didn't know what it was. And then we did.

I was finally diagnosed in my twenties. My problem finally had a name. Tourettes. It also had a duration. Forever. It was never going to go away. I was never going to get "better". This was what I had, and I was who I was. And the voices in my head joined in. Get over it. Get on with it. Suck it up. And, most of all, never let them see you cry. Which was difficult, because crying was pretty much all I felt like doing.

For anyone who does not know or understand what living with Tourettes is like – which is pretty much everyone who does not actually have it – please allow me to explain. It is as if you have just guzzled down four or five heavily caffeinated high sugar soft drinks, followed by the same number of double strength espressos. Next, you slobber on your fingers and stick them into an electrical outlet. Keep them there until your hair starts to smoke. Welcome to my world.

Each of these episodes has a beginning, a middle, and an end. For me, they are usually caused by stress. If I am becoming nervous or anxious, I am guaranteed to spend the next few hours, or few days, experiencing the sensations I just described to you. And doesn't that sound like fun!

For others, their triggers can be any number of things. While it is generally accepted that stress, excitement, and fatigue can aggravate Tourettes episodes, there are numerous other factors that also may do so, including our environment.

In general, environmental factors include what we eat, see, hear, breathe, drink, touch, smell, and otherwise come in contact with. They can even include temperature and lighting. Health issues such as vaccines, medications, viruses, and bacterial infections, can all contribute to precipitating an "outbreak" of tics, and twitches, and sounds, and – yes – even swearing.

Coprolalia: the involuntary use of obscene language and swearing in public.

Not everyone with Tourettes is compelled to swear uncontrollably. Some of us just do it for fun. Seriously, it is a relatively small percentage of people with Tourettes who swear, and yet it is the image that most people have of the condition. That is how we are all too often portrayed on film and television. As a consequence, almost everyone I meet asks the same question, "Why do people like you need to swear?"

The truth is, most of us don't. Only about one in ten. If you figure that about one percent of the population has Tourettes, and only ten percent of those of us who have Tourettes also suffer from coprolalia, it means that it is only one tenth of one percent of the population who does this.

So, the next person you see walking down the street swearing like a sailor is probably not coping with Tourettes. He is just having a bad day.

I am, most fortunately, not one of that small percentage. If I was, my twelve year career as a public speaker would not have lasted twelve seconds. Yes, I am one of the lucky ones. Those of us who live with the non-swearing variety, often refer to our swearing brothers and sisters as having "Full Blown Tourettes", and we feel their pain.

Swearing, and shrieking, and gesturing wildly, does have a tendency to get you noticed. And not in a good way. This type of behaviour goes against every social expectation there is. To say it is frowned upon, would be to painfully understate the response most people have to encountering someone with full-blown Tourettes.

In previous centuries many believed that we were possessed by demons and they burned us at the stake. They don't do that anymore. But, the reactions from some people can seem just as bad.

Imagine for a moment, that you are a young person just trying to fit in. You want to make friends. Ask someone out on a date. Or accept an offer that someone has made to you. Maybe you have gone for your Driver's Test, or a job interview. And each and every moment of this time, you are living in dread that you will have an episode. That you will start twitching. Shrieking. Swearing. How would you like to be that young person? Or that middle-aged man? Or that mother with children?

In some extreme cases, people living with full-blown Tourettes have undergone the type of surgery often associated with cheap horror movies. They have had electrodes permanently placed deep within their brains. These electrodes are attached to something very much like a cardiac pacemaker.

Connected to this controller, the electrodes deliver micro bursts of electricity into the limbic area of the brain. For them, this has been a life saver. Before the surgery, they were being driven mad by the constant twitching and swearing and painful contortions. Now, while not completely free of the symptoms, they are able to live much more complete and fulfilling lives.

Coprolalia, however, is not the only manifestation of Tourettes Syndrome. There is also; Echolalia, which means repeating other people's sounds or speech; Echopraxia, which means repeating other people's gestures or movements; and Palilalia, which is similar to echolalia but involves someone repeating their own sounds or speech. And this only scratches the surface.

One of the more interesting things about Tourettes, is that it is uniquely expressed. No two of us twitch alike. To the casual observer it may seem as if we all have the same kind of twitches, but if you look more closely you will begin to see the differences.

For example, all of my movements occur on the right side of my body. Not the left. Never the left. I have yet to find another twitchy person who manifests his or her Tourettes in this way. For each of us, our tics and twitches and the bizarre movements and odd sounds we make are just our – quite natural – way of expressing our anxiety and stress.

It is the release mechanism, however troubling it may be for both us and the people around us, for the pain and the pressures that build up in our brains. It works for "normal" people too. There was a study conducted that placed test subjects arms in ice cold water for up to ten minutes.

On the first session, the subjects were told to try and stay as still as possible and only use "socially acceptable" words, such as "ouch" and "damn". The next day, the test subjects returned and, once again, had their arms submerged in ice cold water.

This time, however, they were told that they could move the rest of their bodies in any way that felt appropriate, and they could shout or scream or, yes, even swear as much as they wanted. Every single one of the test subjects stated that they were able to endure the pain more easily and longer, when they were allowed to move and swear. These actions enabled them to express, sublimate, or even release the pain they were experiencing, in much the same way as when we twitch.

It is, however, all too easy to get caught up in, and focus on, the drama that is the audio/visual representation of Tourettes. The wildly bizarre movements and the unusual, and often disturbing, sounds are nothing more than the outward expressions of what we are feeling inside. The anxiety, the depression, the obsessive/compulsive thoughts. The confusion, the doubts, the fears that fill our days. Our lives.

It is this "hidden" aspect of Tourettes that is often the hardest with which to cope. Sure it can be embarrassing, for us and those around us, to have to deal with the sounds and movements associated with Tourettes, but it is the constant and unrelenting pressure within us that is the most difficult to bear.

That, and the knowledge that, no matter how much they may love and accept us, no one in our lives truly understands what we are going through. Sound familiar?

I am certain that many of you, probably most of you, feel this way. Maybe every once in a while. Maybe every day. Thanks to the busy lives we lead, we are subjected to almost constant change and extraordinary challenges. Our levels of frustration and anxiety are continually being raised and raised again. Life is hard. All of us are struggling to make it through another day. Stress is virtually – no, actually – killing us. But what are we supposed to do about it?

First, we have to admit – if only to ourselves – that this is what is happening to us. Denial is one of the biggest problems and it is very difficult to overcome. In many ways, I consider myself fortunate to be living with Tourettes. For me, denial was never an option.

I could not simply hide my problems away. They were out there for the whole world to see. All I could do, was face them. And, having done so, try and figure out a way to cope with them. Better yet, to turn them into an advantage. Turn my weakness into strength.

This, of course, is nowhere as easy as it sounds. It took me a very long time, to get even the smallest of handles on it. And I know that it will never change. I know that I will have to keep working at it for the rest of my life. Once I accepted this, things got better. A little. It will never be easy, but I now know that I can control myself. Not what is happening to me. I will never be able to do that. Nobody can.

All we can ever hope to do, is control how we feel about, and therefore react to, what is happening to us. But how do we do that?

There is a wonderful quote by Albert Einstein. It states: "We cannot solve our problems with the same thinking we used when we created them."

I love this quote for two reasons. First, it reminds us that we created the problem in the first place. Maybe we didn't actually create the circumstances, but we certainly chose to be negatively affected by them. And second, it reinforces that we have to change the way we are thinking, or we will never be able to get beyond the problems we have in our lives and begin to become Unstoppable.

The first thing that you have to do, is tell the voices in your head to SHUT UP! Remember, these are the voices you listened to, that got you into this mess in the first place. They are other people's voices. Your parents. Your teachers. Well intentioned friends and lovers.

These are the voices that have told you how to evaluate your situation and determine how you should respond. This is the thinking that created the problems you have. Now it is time to change that. To start to listen to your own voice. How? Easy, just put the car into neutral.

What? Okay, you might need a little more information here. First, try and think of your mind – your thoughts – as a car. Now, picture yourself putting the gear shift of that car into neutral. Not drive. Not reverse. Neutral. Take the load off the engine. Lift your foot off the gas. Stop revving the motor.

Take a breath and try to look at the situation as it is. Not as how somebody else is telling you it is. Not how you wish it was, but how it actually is. However unpleasant that may be. Look at it.

Obviously, we are not cars, but the same theory can apply. Over the years, I have learned how to shift my mind, my thinking, into "Neural Neutral".

Instead of constantly fighting against my Tourettes, and allowing that fight to exhaust me, I am now able to disconnect myself from the physical and emotional stress of the situation. I shift into neutral and step back from the situation. Now I can dispassionately observe and evaluate whatever is happening, without assigning any judgement of positive or negative to it. It simply is what is happening.

By removing all of the old expectations that come from reactive judgement, I am able to see the situation clearly and determine my response accordingly. The panic I used to feel, whenever faced with this kind of situation, simply drops away and I am free to respond to the situation and not how the situation makes me feel. Panic no longer controls my thinking. Now, my thinking controls my panic.

This is huge. If you get nothing else from this book, please try to understand and incorporate this information into your thinking. Into your life.

Panic is a parasite. It feeds off of you. It loves to come at you when you least expect it and hit you in your most vulnerable places. But it needs you to keep it alive. It desperately needs the energy you give it to survive. If you stop feeding it, it will die.

Panic attacks are entirely fear based. They are not real. They exist only in your head. In your thoughts. In the training you have had. So, if you were trained by others to panic, you can train yourself to not. Speaking of trains, that is not a bad analogy.

If you think of panic as a train – a big old freight train – bearing down at you at impossibly high speed, all you have to do is remember that trains run on tracks. Take away the tracks and the train will crash and burn. End of story.

The "Panic Express" runs on the tracks we built. We had help, of course, but we built them. Which means we can destroy them. Destroy them, and you will regain your freedom from panic. You were not born to panic. It is something you have learned. So, unlearn it.

Learn instead to derail your panic attacks and regain dominion over your life. Once panic is gone from your reality, you can easily select better actions. New options, new ideas, new choices can be made and implemented.

Okay, but how do you do that? Where do you start? Well, for me it came right in the middle of the worst panic attack of my life. I was driving in my car, on my way from one speaking engagement to another. I was on my way from Portland to San Francisco. It was an absolutely gorgeous day. Bright, sunny, perfect.

And right out of the blue, it hit me like the Titanic hit the iceberg. One minute I am dancing in the ballroom and then, suddenly, I am clinging next to Leo in the freezing water. I will never forget how it felt. All the colour drained out of my surroundings. Everything became grey.

Every positive thought I had been having disappeared and I was left with nothing but sorrow and sadness. My beautiful day was gone and I was once again surrounded by the demons of my past. But, this time, I was not going to let them win. I did something I had never done before. This time, I did not cry. This time, I smiled.

That's right. I started to smile. Not a winsome little smile, like a shy schoolgirl. No, this was a full on Jack Nicholson's Joker sized smile. I smiled until my face hurt. And I just kept smiling.

Oh sure, the voices in my head were having a field day. "What are you, crazy?" "You should be crying!" "Don't you realize that your life is meaningless and you are worthless?" "Stop smiling!" My subconscious was going a little nuts. It could not figure out what was happening. I shouldn't be smiling. That is not how this is supposed to work.

My conscious mind, however, stepped up. It told my subconscious that everything was fine and that there was no reason for all of these feelings of doom and dread.

And, just like that, it all changed. It was almost as if my subconscious mind had apologised. It was as if it was sorry for raising a false alarm. It had realised that nothing was actually wrong and it would simply shut up and mind its own business.

In that very instant, I knew that panic attacks would never be a problem again. And they haven't been. To this day, more than ten years later, these debilitating panic attacks have never returned. One simple thing had made all the difference. A smile.

I realize that not all of you might suffer from panic attacks, but there is definitely something that is holding you back from becoming Unstoppable. Once you have identified it, you can begin to change it. It will take time. It won't be easy. But it can be done. Just keep smiling.

CHAPTER 10

Shake hands with the Devil

I am sure that a few of you – probably more than a few – have begun to think, "This fella must be crazy!"

"Smile? I am having the worst (fill in the blank) of my life, and he wants me to smile. I can't do that."

Yeah, I do. And, yes, you can. It is simply another choice that you get to make. Sure, you can cry if you want to, but how has that been working out for you? Or, you can slap that big, cheesy grin on your face and get on with doing whatever you need to do to get past this moment. Just remember to breathe.

I am serious here. Most people, at moments of extreme stress and tension, simply stop breathing. Now, in addition to the problem that you already had, your body thinks you are dying and tries to kick-start the system.

Adrenalin floods through your bloodstream. Your heart starts to race. You break out in a sweat. You get cold, or hot, or dizzy, or nauseous, or all of them at the same time. Now you have two problems. The cause. And the effect.

The worst part of it is, that you cannot even begin to solve the first problem, until you solve the second. If you can't get yourself back to yourself, you can't use all of the amazing resources you have inside you to solve the problem that started this mess in the first place.

I realize that this is nowhere as easy as it sounds but, like using any other tool, things do get better with practice. The first few times you try and use any tool, it feels awkward and clumsy.

The results are seldom perfect. But, you kept at it and it got better, easier. The same is true with this. Just keep doing it. Over and over and over again. Don't worry, life will give you plenty of opportunities to practice.

The minute you start to feel the situation get away from you. The second you start to respond physically to the situation. The moment all of the fears and frustrations you have tried to keep locked away, come crashing through the door. Stop. Take a deep breath. Take another one. Now . . . smile.

First of all, this needs to be the biggest smile you can possibly make. An ear to ear, cheek burning, jaw cracking, smile. A, "I just won the lottery!" smile. Second, you have to concentrate. On your breathing – slow, steady, even – and on holding this enormous smile for as long as you can. Then, hold it a little longer.

What is happening is both simple and profound. First of all, you are now in charge of the situation. At least in terms of how you are reacting to it. Remember, we cannot always control what is happening around us, but we do have the ability to control what is happening to us. Second, you are sending a very clear, and strong, message to the rest of your body.

"Sure, something might be wrong outside, but – look at the face – everything seems to be okay up there, so go ahead and turn off the alarm."

Now, a lot of people might confuse this with the old "grin and bear it" school of thought. And they would be right, if that is where you choose to stop. Forcing yourself to smile. Making the choice to address the situation in this new and unusual manner, will help for the moment.

It will allow you to step back and more accurately assess the situation. It takes the heat out of the moment. Which is vitally important. When you are in the middle of the situation, all you can think about is how it is making you feel. It is a surprisingly complex combination of brain functions.

Inside our tiny little heads, there is a lot going on. Our Reptilian Brain, the oldest part of the human brain, is trying to cope with all of the signals coming at it. Positive or negative, it will respond by trying to control physical responses. Breathing, heartrate, hormones, etc. are all controlled from here.

Now, if you have been paying attention, you probably noticed that I said "signals". What signals? The signals coming at the Reptilian Brain, are coming from the Limbic Brain. The what?

The Limbic Brain first appeared in mammals. This part of our brains records the memories of our experiences – good or bad – so it is responsible for our emotions. The Limbic Brain is where emotional value judgements are made, often completely unconsciously, and it exerts an incredibly strong influence on our Reptilian Brains and, therefore, our physical responses to situations – especially stressful ones.

Last, but absolutely not least, is the Neocortex. The Neocortex first developed in the primates and evolved, over considerable time, into the human brain as we know it today.

The two large central hemispheres that form such an important part of our Cerebral Cortex, are responsible for language, imagination, and consciousness. The truly great thing about this part of our brains, is that it is incredibly flexible and has infinite learning capacity. It also, with your permission, can be the "Boss".

Okay, what I mean by that is actually very simple. This is the part of the brain that "thinks". Remember, the Limbic Brain is responsible for "feeling" and the Reptilian Brain just does what it is told. So, unless you use the Neocortex to control the situation, your emotions will run your body off a cliff. Or, in my case, almost off a balcony.

However, if you can somehow manage to encourage the "thinking" part of your brain to get over, around, or past the "feeling" part of your brain, you will be able to gain at least some control over your body. For example: Something has just happened that has triggered a reaction within you.

Maybe it relates to a bad memory, or it pushes some button that was installed by others when you were a child. Immediately, you begin to have a negative physical reaction to the situation. Your body begins to get out of your control.

The moment this starts, what you need to do is stop the process. This is where you smile. You consciously force yourself to react in a manner inconsistent with your emotions and, therefore, counter to the signals being sent through to the ancient portion of your brain.

Your body gets confused. "Am I happy or sad?" "Am I getting ready to punch this person, or give him a hug?" "What the heck is going on here?"

In this moment, you're now in control of your response. You may not be in control of the actual situation, but you are in control of how it is making you feel. From this point on, you can start to think your way through the problem.

Is it easy? No. Is it possible? Yes. How do I know? I do it every day. That day in the car, I learned that I was in control. Not of the world and everything that happens in it, but over how I was going to react to what happens in this world.

Instead of letting the fear and the anxiety control my life, I was going to spend my life controlling the fear and the anxiety.

Notice that I said "the" and not "my" just then. The fear. Not my fear. The anxiety. Not my anxiety. I refuse to own those things anymore.

Sure, I still come across situations that trigger these things, but now I do something very different from what I used to do. I do the opposite. I don't cry. I smile. I don't pull back. I move forward. I don't hide myself away. I stand up on a stage and talk to hundreds of people at a time. And I, most assuredly, don't stand on a balcony and do anything other than admire the view.

There is an interesting thing, by the way, about standing on balconies, or any high and exposed place for that matter. Most people are not actually afraid of falling to their deaths. Most people are afraid they will jump. As weird as that sounds, it is true. Left to their own devices, our bodies can do a pretty good job of keeping us safe and healthy. It is not a natural physical response to jump from a high place, whenever the situation presents itself. We were not designed that way.

Our bodies want to survive. They will do incredible things to keep working. There are countless stories about people who experienced terrible physical hardship and are still with us. It happens every day.

There are, quite sadly, also countless stories about other people who seemed to have everything going for them and yet they chose to jump from their own high place. They overran their own body's desire to survive. They took control and stepped over the edge.

What is most tragic about this, is that it proves that they were capable of controlling their actions. They were capable of making a choice. They did not simply react to their situation, they acted upon it. I know what this feels like. I made my choice. I make it every day.

I am sure that many of you are making that choice – the choice to step away from the edge – each and every day as well. But, what if we never got to the edge, at all?

I have called this chapter, "Shake hands with the Devil". What I mean by that is very simple. You have to stand face to face with whatever it is in your life that is preventing you from becoming Unstoppable and reach out and take it by the hand.

Notice I did not say "whoever". This is not about somebody else. It is about you. It does not matter, even in the slightest, who did what to you. I am sorry that it happened. Whatever it was. And I join you in your condemnation of the person who did this to you. Whoever it was. But this is not about them. It is not even about what they did. It is about what you are continuing to do to yourself because of it. This is about the choices you have made.

So, stand up and take a good hard look. At the fear. At the anxiety. At the insecurity. At the sense of self-loathing and shame. Look the Devil in the eye, reach for his hand, and shake his hand "Goodbye". Tell him that you just won't be needing him around anymore. It can be done. There are lots of ways to do it, but it most definitely can be done.

I have only shared the following story with a few close friends. And a room full of two hundred Clinical Psychologists. The story begins in my childhood.

Every morning, as I walked out of our front door, to go to school, I felt as if I had a big ball of string hung from my back. With every step I took, a little of this string would unwind. The farther I walked, the more string was strung out behind me. I swear that I could actually feel people walking on it and cars driving over it.

Once I was at school, I would walk from class to class, always retracing my steps so that I could gather the string back up. I wasn't always able to do this, and every time that happened, I felt like the string would break. This was horrible, because I also felt that, if I could not keep the string in one piece, my Mother would die some unspeakable death.

If this had happened only once, it would have been terrifying, but this happened each and every day. Exactly the same. Every time. It became the central focus of my days. I had to do everything I could, anything I could, to keep the string in one piece. Otherwise my Mother would die. And each time I failed, I was convinced that she had. I knew, beyond doubt, that my failure had killed my Mother. My failure had caused her dreadful suffering. Over and over again. Endlessly.

I never told anyone. I was only eight years old, but I had already learned that I couldn't. Nobody was going to believe me. I was alone. And no matter how many days I came home and found my Mother still alive, I knew that tomorrow would be different.

Tomorrow she would die. This continued for three years. Then it changed. As suddenly as this nightmare had come upon me, it left. But it hadn't. Not really.

For over forty years, that terrified little eight year old boy lived buried deep inside me. The man I had become, kept the boy I had been, safely hidden behind walls of silence. His fears no longer controlled my life. Or so I thought. Until that day.

I was speaking in front of an audience of Clinical Psychologists in Texas. Yes, they have psychologists in Texas! I was telling them about my experiences, and the difficulty, of living with Tourettes and OCD.

Much to my surprise, I found myself telling them the story of the little boy with the big ball of string. I do not totally remember everything I said that day, but I do remember the standing ovation I received, and the overwhelming outpouring of support and encouragement they gave to me.

They had heard my pain, and for that they sympathized, but they had also heard my strength, and for that they applauded. That same experience is waiting for you. You don't need an audience of two hundred people, of course, just an audience of one. You.

You have something in your life that is restricting you, restraining you, keeping you locked in and unable to get past your past. Maybe it is one thing. Maybe it is many.

Whatever it is, it is holding you back from being Unstoppable, and you have to let it go. You have to take it by the hand and say, "Goodbye". Once and for all.

So, find yourself some quiet place. Sit down. And tell yourself the story. Be honest. Be exacting. Be thorough. And be ready. This is going to kick up a lot of dust. I guarantee you there will be tears. And, if you are at all like me, a lot of snot and the odd moan or two. Just stick with it. Finish the story. Stop. Breathe. Smile.

Step past the emotions and think about what had happened and the control it has had over your life. Think about how you have let the past take control of your present. Get mad. Stomp around. Swear. Break something cheap and easily replaced. Stop. Breathe. Smile.

Now, you are ready. You can see clearly what you have been doing and why. You can see what has been holding you back and why. You can see what you have to do to change your life. And why.

The "how" will come. You will learn what you need to do to deal with the old feelings. You will learn how to experience the new ones.

All that matters for now, is that you have learned "why". The hardest part of effecting any change, is the understanding of why you have to change in the first place. Understanding "why" is the first step.

As for my little eight year old self, he didn't miraculously go away. He is still around. I see him every once in a while. In his own way, he is kind of cute. I love him. Not because of who he was, but because of who I have become. Not in spite of. Because of. His weaknesses have become my strengths. His fears have become my focus.

I don't know what it is that is holding you back. I don't even want to guess. But I am pretty sure that there is something. You are a little too far into this book for it to be just simple curiosity. So, it is time to find out what it is. Do what I suggested. Invite your demons to tea and take a good long look at them and what you have allowed them to do to your life. Go through the steps. Be courageous. Above all, be honest.

Just remember this. Unless you have a definable, diagnosable mental illness, that affects your ability to perceive the reality of the world around you, everything that plagues you; everything that is causing you to be less than you can be; everything that is preventing you from becoming Unstoppable; came to you from someone else.

It was given to you and you decided to keep it. You chose to let it control your life. Your happiness. Even your health. And you can choose to stop letting it do that. At the very least, you can stop helping.

Do yourself a favor and read back a couple of chapters. Go back over the information about Selective Perception and reinforce your awareness of what it does to you. I am sure some of you are feeling its forces right now. If all of this is making you uncomfortable, even a little bit, it is happening. And it is about to get worse.

CHAPTER 11

You don't know what you don't know

In the last chapter, I mentioned "diagnosable" mental illness. Being able to get a clear cut, well defined, statement of fact from a qualified professional. Good luck with that.

The sad fact of the matter, is that mental illness is very difficult to diagnose, at least accurately. I am sure that you have heard the saying, "Life is a banquet". Well, mental illness is a buffet. It is almost always a little bit of this and a little bit of that.

The truly important thing to know, is that it can and will affect all of us at some point in our life. I am not saying that you have, or will develop, a mental illness, but I guarantee you that you already know someone who is currently struggling with one.

A friend, a family member, a co-worker, your Boss (you always suspected, didn't you), somebody in your life is facing challenges you do not know about.

As I already stated, Tourettes affects about 1% of the general population, but there's a lot more out there. Schizophrenia affects about the same percentage of the population as Tourettes, but Anxiety Disorder affects more than 5%. Depression raises the bar to 8%.

In fact, if you put the numbers all together, at least one out of five people in North America will suffer from a mental condition at some point during his or her life. Yet only one out of those five will ever be diagnosed or receive treatment for the condition.

Think about those numbers for a second. If you were in a room of one hundred people, statistically speaking at least twenty of them would have some sort of mental condition and, of those twenty, only four of them has ever been diagnosed or received any treatment. The rest of them have no idea why they feel the way they do. They do not know what is "wrong" with them. And the odds are, they never will.

This is a tragedy for all of us, not just them. The numbers are staggering. In Canada alone, almost 5% of all general hospital admissions are for mental health conditions. That amounts to over 2,000,000 hospital days of care in one country alone. A country with a relatively small population and a fairly accessible health care system. The cost in dollars is overwhelming, but the cost in lives is worse.

It is not unreasonable to assume that mental illness plays a significant part in many, if not most, of the suicides that occur every year. And the numbers for suicide are large and ever growing. 24% of all deaths between the ages of 15 and 24. 16% between the ages of 24 and 44. Again, these are Canadian statistics from a few years back, but it is highly likely that these are small numbers by comparison to the rest of the world.

The saddest part of this, is that – for most of us – we never even think about it until it happens to us, or to some celebrity. Like most of us, I loved, and will always miss, Robin Williams. How tragic is it, that a man who gave us so much joy, had so little in his own life? More tragic still, is there is probably someone you know who, at this very moment, is considering suicide as a way to end the pain and misery that fills the endless days and even longer nights, and you will only know about it after it has happened.

I once heard a professor of psychology refer to suicide as a "symptom" of mental illness and, while this is certainly possible, it does not leave us any room for action. This may be the worst thing about knowing someone who has committed suicide.

The idea that we might have been able to do something, anything, if only we had known. But, we didn't. And we don't. And we probably never will.

Nobody knew what was going on in my head. Not from the age of eight. Not at any point in my life. Certainly not on that horrible/beautiful day I stood on my balcony and seriously considered stepping over the edge. Nobody knew what was going on in my head. Just as nobody knows what is going on in yours.

I believe that we are all programmed to hide our weaknesses. Maybe it is simply nature at work. The strong survive, the weak are lunch. Maybe it is training. Focus on the positives, ignore the negatives. Maybe it is nothing more than wishful thinking. If you fake it, you will make it.

Whatever it is, it is likely stopping you from ever finding out what is really happening inside your head. And, without that knowledge and awareness, everything else just gets harder and harder.

When I finally was diagnosed, it was not as if a great weight had been lifted from my shoulders – that weight is there and it is never going away – it was just that I now had something I could use to start to try and understand what was happening. Why I was doing what I was doing. Overnight, I went from being just a weirdo, to being a person with a mental illness. It helped me, more than I can ever say, to feel better about myself.

I was convinced, however, that it would make it worse if other people knew. I had had enough trouble from them when they just thought I was "strange". What would they do if they thought I was "crazy"?

I tried, for all too many years, to keep my problems to myself. Sure, people could see what I was doing – the twitching is pretty hard to hide – but I never would explain what was happening to me. I would simply try harder to control what was happening around me, so that I could have more control over what was happening inside me.

I became relentless in my efforts to be so good at everything I did, that the twitching would either go un-noticed, or it wouldn't matter to whomever I was with. When I became a professional public speaker, it became worse. I was convinced that no one would ever hire me if they knew and that they would never have me back if they saw me in all my twitchy glory. I could not have been more wrong.

Today, all of my meeting planner clients and friends – the people who write the cheques – call me "Twitchy" and they are thrilled to book me again and again. What used to set me aside, now sets me apart. I have taken those things I so relentlessly tried to hide and now I use those very things to continue to build my Unstoppable life. I also try to help others, who either have Tourettes or have someone in their life who does.

Most of the parents I have met, feel understandably distressed when their perfect little son or daughter starts to twitch. Often they blame themselves. They assume that the issue is behavioral and, therefore, was something that they instilled. While this is often true of many behaviors, it is not true of Tourettes or any other mental illness.

Tourettes, like many of the dozens of other definable mental conditions, does not show itself at birth. It hides deep inside the mind of the child and only shows itself later, as they mature.

It is also so very easy to miss the symptoms. Many of the obvious warning signs of mental illness can be passed off as almost anything but. It is perfectly acceptable to not know what you don't know, but the problems occurs when you don't see what you don't want to see.

It is very difficult, I know, for a parent to come face to face with the issue of mental illness in a child. Shame. Blame. Fear. Despair. All of these prey on the peace of mind of a parent with a mentally ill child. And why wouldn't it? Every parent wants the best for their child and this certainly isn't that. What kind of life could this child possibly have?

This is where the parent – maybe you – gets to make a very important choice. Face up to the reality of the problem, or turn away in denial and begin a life of wishing and hoping. And, just in case you need to be reminded, neither a wish nor a hope, is a plan. And a plan is what you desperately need.

You need a direction. And that direction needs to be creating an environment where the child, every child, gets to reach his or her full potential. Whatever that may look like.

The first thing you need to do, is give yourself a break. You didn't cause this. It is not your fault. It is an illness. So, cut yourself some slack. At least in the "blame" department. You have other areas where your energies and efforts are much more needed. Remember the analogy of the airplane oxygen mask? Put yours on first.

A short time ago, I met a mother whose son had recently been diagnosed with Tourettes. She had attended one of my Keynote addresses in Edmonton. She was understandably upset, but she was determined to do what was best for her son. She wanted to talk with me about Tourettes, but I knew that first she had to find some peace with what was happening. To her son. To her.

I looked into her eyes and said this:

"You are a wonderful person. You love your son and he loves you. Forgive yourself. Forgive yourself right now. Why? Because, there is actually nothing to forgive. There is no way you caused this. There is no way you could have known that this would happen to your son. This isn't your fault, any more than it is his. And don't worry.

Look at me. Closely. I am in my fifties. I am happily married. I live well. I love. I laugh. I travel the world. I own my own company and, before that, I worked with some of the world's leading companies. Those same opportunities exist for your son. With your help.

Look into my eyes and listen with all your heart. Let go of the fear. Let go of the anger. Just let it go. Right here. Right now. Just let it go.

Your son has the most important thing he needs to make this work. To build a life for himself. A life that any mother would be proud of seeing for her child. He has you."

Quite naturally, she broke down. I did not ask her to stop crying. I asked her to cry more. I encouraged her to freely express all of the emotions that had been raging through her. I held her as this torrent of emotions ran its course. Until she calmed and she was able to smile again.

Now, this happened in front of a group of people, some of the others who had been at my presentation, and nobody turned away. Nobody was embarrassed or frightened by what they had seen. Many of them were openly crying as well. Even if they did not understand her situation, they had been touched by her pain. And her strength.

This was our experience that day and it has been my experience every time something like this has occurred.

People are, for the most part, kind. As merciless and hurtful as the children in my past had been, the adults I have met have been understanding and supportive. Some are fascinated by my condition. Many have stories of their own issues to share. Others just want to know more about how they can become Unstoppable. After all, if a guy like twitchy old me can do it . . .

It is always difficult to face up to mental illness. For a parent, it often feels as if their child has actually died. They start to mourn for the life their child has now lost and will never regain. For an adult, receiving a personal diagnosis of mental illness, it often leaves you feeling lost and alone. Nobody else will understand. Nobody else will care.

I remember that feeling. I will never forget it. I just no longer allow it to control my life. I will live the life of my own choosing. I am now, and I will always be, Unstoppable.

It has been a long journey and it was not an easy one. You know something about my early years, and quite a bit about my life now, but you don't know about the day I finally was able to name my problem. I was twenty one years old and living in Medicine Hat, Alberta. I was happily working fourteen hour shifts as a roughneck out in the oil fields. Good money. Good times. I was "funny old Stu".

I had lots of friends and they liked me. One of them liked me enough to tell me what he thought was wrong with me.

I suppose that I had become inured to the oddity of my behavior over the years. I was still quite uncomfortable with some of the more overwhelming aspects of my condition, but I was dealing with it. I was working at a job I liked. I was living a life I enjoyed. I didn't need some well-intentioned "know it all" telling me what was wrong with me. But, a part of me needed to hear it, so I listened.

What he said made sense. So I went to a doctor and he confirmed the diagnosis. My condition had a name . . . Tourettes. I had never heard of it. I didn't know anything about it. All I knew is what the doctor told me. I had it and it was never going to go away.

Tourettes is incurable. Most mental illnesses are. They are never going to go away. Even if you do not have a mental illness, those things that cause you pain, those things that keep you sleepless and afraid, those things that are keeping you from realizing your full potential, those things are most likely never to go away either.

All you can hope to do – and this you most certainly can do – is find a way to live with them. Not give in to them. Not give up and just accept a diminished life because of them. No. That is not what I am suggesting.

What I am talking about, is taking control of those feelings and finding ways in which to cope with those things that trigger the fear, and the anxiety, and the depression, and the despair. Find the buttons that the world has installed and then find ways in which to reduce the impact they have on your life, whenever somebody accidentally, or deliberately, pushes one of them. And, yes, people do like pushing them. Especially when they were the ones who installed them.

This is one of the things that makes this undertaking so difficult for most people. They are surrounded by people who, regardless of the difficulties you are facing in your life, simply do not want you to change. They know you. They like you. They control you.

What? How do they control me? Simple. By "accepting" you for who and what you are, they are discouraging you from ever changing. This would be fine, if you were actually who and what you wanted to be, but are you? Are you everything you want to be? Probably not.

First of all, are you Unstoppable? Do you know where you want to go? Do you know how to get there? Do you know what your "perfect" life even looks like? Or have you been pushing any thoughts about those things deeper and deeper down inside you, because to even think about them for a moment causes you discomfort?

The odds are pretty good that this is exactly what you have been doing. It is understandable. We were all raised to be good little boys and girls. To do as our elders told us, because they knew better. Well, look around you. This is the life that you built on the foundation they gave you. What do you think of it so far?

Look, I am not trying to be unkind here. I am not deliberately trying to insult your parents, or your friends, or your loved ones. Let's give them the benefit of the doubt, and say that they "meant" well. But, meaning well does not guarantee doing well. And if you are not satisfied in your life. If you are not happy in your life. If you are not living the life you want and need to. If you are not Unstoppable. You are quite simply NOT doing "well", at least not well enough.

So, change it. How? Try a few of the things I am suggesting. Most of all, take a real hard look at yourself. Get to know you. And then take yourself out for a walk. Out the door. Down the street. Into the nearest group therapy session you can find. Wait a minute! What? "Therapy. I don't need therapy." Well, maybe you do. Maybe you don't. I don't know. But what I do know is this. For any of this to work, you need to start changing perceptions. Your own. And those of the people around you. You need to start finding yourself. And this is never going to happen if the only feedback you get is from people who have a vested interest in you staying exactly the same as you are.

CHAPTER 12

Who in the world am I?

I seriously doubt that there is a single person out there, who has not asked this question at least once in his or her life. It is the most natural question in the world to ask. To yourself. To others. And this is where the problem begins. Even if you have not actually voiced this question to others, their answers to it come at you constantly.

All of us are bombarded with input, from a variety of sources, which tells us who we should be. Our family. Our religion. Our culture. These are the sources of "direct" control over our self-image. These forces provide us with the rules around which we are expected to live our lives. We learn these rules from a very early age. We learn through observation. We are deliberately taught them by others. And we believe them because we have nothing with which to measure their validity.

As we grow, we begin to find new and different sources of information. Now friends become a major source of new rules. Peer pressure is one of the most powerful – and insidious – forces in a person's life.

It starts in the earliest grades in school and continues throughout our lives. We eventually trade class-mates for co-workers, but the demand that we modify or manufacture behavior, or thought, remains ever present and ever powerful.

These are the sources of Direct Influence. Constantly answering the question, even if you never asked it.

And if you do ask it, "Who am I?" More often than not, they will instead tell you "what" you are. My son. My daughter. My friend. A doctor. A lawyer. A teacher.

Seldom will they address the essential humanity in the question. Certainly they are not interested in addressing the individuality in it. The obvious answer they want you to hear is, "You are just like us." This is both a confirmation and a command. If you follow our rules, you can remain one of us. Don't, and the world you know could be taken from you. There is an enormous price to be paid for independence. For individuality. It is all about power. Theirs.

Indirect Influence is even more prevalent. It is literally in the air around us. Movies. Television. The Internet. Advertisements for everything from air freshener to automobiles. From bathroom tissue to beachfront resorts. Politics. Patriotism. And, most of all, pain.

If you were an alien from some far and distant planet, who had just arrived on earth, and your only source of information about humans as a species was advertising, you would be convinced that we are the biggest bunch of sissies in the universe. We seem to be constantly searching for a way to avoid feeling anything unpleasant. Ever.

Is this necessarily a bad thing? It is far too easy to say, "No." Obviously, no healthy person enjoys pain, so anything that will take it away must be good. Right? Not really. Pain is the way our bodies tell us to not do whatever it is we are doing. It is a signal that something is wrong. This is as true of psychological pain, as it is of physical. We need to feel pain in order to ensure that what we are doing is right for us. Put your finger in the fire. It hurts. Take your finger out. It stops. It all seems pretty simple doesn't it?

But, what if you were trying to reach through the fire to take hold of something wonderful? Something of value beyond measure. Perhaps, something that you need to survive. Would it be worth a little pain – and a pretty big blister – to get all of that? For far too many people, the answer is a resounding, "NO".

Many philosophers throughout history, from Aristotle to Bentham to Tony Robbins, have all said the same thing. There are two dynamic forces in human existence; the desire to gain pleasure and the need to avoid pain. And of these two, the avoidance of pain is the most compelling. Any type of pain.

We will do anything to not hurt. Even change our lives. In fact, that may be what we choose to do first. And, in making that choice, we never learn what we could have become.

In many ways, I must say that I am grateful for having Tourettes. As odd as this might sound, I know that I would not be the person I am today, if I had not had to find ways to live in this world because of, in spite of, Tourettes.

Now, I am not suggesting that I have not wished on occasion that I did not have it, or thought about what my life would have been like if I didn't, but I know I would not have become who I am. I do not know where I would be living, or with whom, and I do not know what I would be doing for a living, but I cannot imagine that I could be any happier or more fulfilled than I am with the life I now have.

Obviously, I can say that now, but if I had been offered, at any point during my teenage years, the opportunity to magically make the Tourettes go away, I know that I would have jumped at it. I would have done anything to avoid any more of the pain it was causing.

And in doing so, I would have also lost all of the pleasure that my life now contains. I am not saying that my problems have all gone away. I still put my hand in the fire quite regularly. And it still hurts. But now I know what I am reaching for and I am prepared to trade a little pain for the incredible amount and variety of the pleasure I gain.

I know this for me and I believe it for you. Yes, you are struggling. I know you are in pain. I know that there are things about your life that you wish you could change. If only. If only what? If only it didn't hurt.

Well, I am sorry to tell you this . . . it is going to hurt. Maybe a little. Probably a lot. There is no possible way to change your life and avoid it being painful. It is simply going to hurt. But, remember this, you are not just putting your hand in the fire for no reason.

You are reaching through the fire to take hold of something precious. You are reaching through the fire to take hold of you. Of your life. As it rightly can be, not merely as you have been told it should.

Here is a very interesting aspect of the pain/pleasure continuum. While it is obvious that pain reduces pleasure. What is not so obvious, is that pleasure reduces pain. Not just metaphorically. Pleasure actually releases hormones that have an analgesic (pain reducing) effect on your body. If you do more things that cause you pleasure, the more the pain will be reduced. This is something you already know.

Alcohol, drugs, sex, reality TV, all can be used to take the pain away. For a moment or two. Of course, after a while you need more and different types and amounts of these "pleasures". Your body stops responding to how much, or how often, and you need more. This is addiction.

Obviously, I am not encouraging you to develop an addiction. In fact, it is just the opposite. Trying to find an "outside" solution to an "inside" problem never ever works. All you end up with, is another problem. You go from being unhappy with your life. To being unhappy with your life and a DUI court case looming in the future.

Yet, this is what most people do. They seek to sublimate their pain, rather than find a way to solve it. You see, pain is not the problem. It is a symptom of the problem. If you can identify the problem and solve it, or at the very least change the way you feel about it, you will diminish, or even eliminate, the pain. You will also open the door to new and better sources of infinite pleasure.

The trouble is, that most of us are like water running downhill. We always try to find the path of least resistance. Understandable. After all, we were taught this by the people who did not want us to resist them. You have all heard the saying, "You have to get along to go along." Meaning, "find a seat, sit down, shut up, hang on, and we will all get there together".

But what if you want to go somewhere else? Why would anyone stay on a bus that is taking them someplace they don't really want to go? No relatively sane person would do that. Wrong.

We do it all the time. Most of us live a life of perpetual procrastination. We know where we want to go. We may even know how to get there. We just can't get up off our backsides and go. For example, I have a weight problem. Not unusual, most of the western world has a problem with weight. We eat too much and move too little. Anyway, I weighed myself a short time ago and I was horrified to see what a big, fat pig I had become.

Now, this did not happen overnight. I had been watching my weight slowly increasing for the last couple of years and, while it did bother me, it wasn't bad enough to do anything about. Until that morning. I looked up from the scale and saw myself in the mirror.

I could no longer deny it. I was fat. Grossly fat. And I hated it. I hated myself for letting this happen. I walked out of the bathroom and told my wife that I was going to diet. Now, I had said this to her probably a hundred times before, but this time it was different. I knew it. I felt it. The pain of seeing what I had done to myself, was far worse than the pain of exercise or denying myself any of the treats I so enjoy.

So, I changed my diet. I began to exercise. I put my hand in the fire. I lost a couple of pounds. Then I lost a few more. And then some more. I also started to feel stronger. Better. Healthier. Now that, and the pleasure of seeing the Adonis I was becoming, had eliminated the pain.

The lesson to be learned from my little story, is very simple. Most of us live, however unwittingly, in a state of constant procrastination. We do so, because we have learned to try and avoid pain at all cost. Partly this is biology, but mostly it is training.

We have learned that it is easier to find ways to avoid pain, than it is to find ways to overcome it and attain pleasure. In a very disturbing way, we actually begin to find pleasure in a controlled and tolerable amount of pain.

This is called Secondary Gain. Sometimes pain will get us a certain amount of pleasure. Not necessarily the pain itself, but things associated with it. It might get us sympathy. Or it might get us out of a responsibility we don't like. Maybe it will get us more or better drugs. Maybe it will do nothing more than to get people to leave us alone.

All of these, and more, can provide a small amount of the pleasure that we are seeking. Without having to do anything about the real problem that is causing the pain. Unfortunately, it keeps you locked in that cycle.

You need to have the pain, in order to get the pleasure that comes, however indirectly, from it. And there you are . . . trapped. You have a job you hate, but the pay is pretty good. You hate your spouse, but the kids are kind of cool. Your parents are tyrants, but you are still named in the will.

So, you end up living a diminished life, because it is easier to put up with the pain you know, instead of trying to change that life and have to face up to a whole new pain that you don't.

After a while, you end up on autopilot. You sit back, abdicating control of your life to the forces around you. Soon, you start to justify your position. You start to blame those around you, or the world in general, for your unhappiness. For your failure to be living the life you want. "I could have been someone, or done something, if only it hadn't been for . . . ". Your parents. Your spouse. Someone else. Anyone else.

Excuses pile up on top of other excuses. Until, pretty soon, we not only don't like the life we have, we stop caring about it. It becomes less and less valuable to us. And then we end up standing on a balcony.

I know that this is how I have felt for most of my life. Until the day I found myself standing on the edge. That horrible/beautiful day that changed my life forever. It took a long time for me to get there but, as I said before, I am a hard learner. Or maybe I just wasn't aware of what I was learning.

The lessons I learned as a child; the rejection and ridicule of my peers; the abuse suffered at the hands of someone who was supposed to love me; the confusion and sadness that came from watching two unhappy parents struggle to find something, anything, that could make their lives more tolerable; all of this had been building a well of strength I did not even imagine I could possess.

I went from being afraid to talk to anyone, to being able to talk with the CEOs of major corporations all over the world. I went from hiding in the corner, to standing at the front of stages before hundreds of people at a time. I went from being unmovable to being Unstoppable.

Tourettes, and all of its associated disorders, will always be with me. I have, however, chosen to stop viewing it as my "weakness" and, instead, view it as the foundation of my success.

I do not know what your weakness is. What irrational fears or irrelevant belief systems, trained into you by others in your past, are holding you back today and preventing you from having the tomorrow of your choosing. All I know, is that they are there. And they can be overcome.

I travel constantly around the world showing others how anyone can turn their old weaknesses into newfound strengths. One of the areas in which I do a lot of work, is International Tourism and this provides a perfect example of what I taking about.

Most of the employees that make up the workforce in tourism related enterprises, are virtually invisible to average customers. Cooks, housekeepers, cleaners, gardeners, pool boys, waitresses, desk clerks, valets, etc.

You might know that they are there, but do you really look at them? Interact with them on any meaningful level? Probably not. Why would you? You are not being unkind, or unfair. They have a job to do.

What is interesting, is that it would all come to a crashing halt without them. Here they are, the lowest paid workers in the industry. Many of them uneducated and unskilled, and yet the entire industry depends on them to do their jobs in the best way possible. Always. And most of them do.

In fact, they often go far above and beyond the minimum expectations that are required. The literally become what I call Front-line Superstars. They routinely "Over Wow".

I love that term. "Over Wow". They don't just do a good job. They do an amazing one. They don't just "wow" you. They "Over Wow". They do more than they need to do, in spite of their lowly positions and inadequate pay. But why? Who would blame them if they didn't? Sure, they need to do enough to not get fired, but why do more?

Maybe it is because that people who are at the bottom, often have a better perspective on what is truly important. There is little, or nothing, that can be done to improve their working conditions or increase their income. There is a great deal, however, that can be done to enable them to feel empowered and enriched.

They do this by going out there, beyond the limits of the physical reality of their positions, into the area of personal responsibility and interaction. They care about the work they do. And they care about the people for whom they do it. Every day, they reach through the fire – the low wages and the staggering workload – and they grasp the most important point of it all. To give.

You see, this is not just about you. Sure, you are important. You are essential. It is vital that you become the best you can be. That you become Unstoppable.

But, you are not just doing this for yourself. You are doing this for each and every person who passes through your life. I don't mean for this to feel like pressure, and I know that your objective is to get moving toward being the person you were meant to be and having the life you truly deserve, but your impact on others is absolutely unavoidable. You know this. It was others who impacted you. Some positively. Others considerably less so.

We have no choice in being an example of some kind and having an impact on those around us, but we do have a choice in the kind of example and impact we provide.

In life, we all get opportunities to do something else. To try something new. To be someone different. Often, we turn away from these opportunities. Out of fear. Out of anxiety. Out of insecurity. It is what we have been trained to do. Now, we need to train ourselves to do the opposite. Not to give up. Not to give in. Not to turn away at the least sign of conflict or confusion.

Simply by choosing to reach through the fire and grab another handful of a new and wonderful future. Soon you will find yourself in the position Lewis Carroll described in Alice in Wonderland, when he wrote, "I can't go back to yesterday because I was a different person then."

One of the best ways to test this hypothesis, is to try one very simple thing. Smile. No, not the huge "Cheshire Cat" grin (to stay with the Lewis Carroll theme for a moment), that I have encouraged you to use to get past moments of crippling anxiety, but a smaller, gentler, but no less effective one. A smile from your heart. From all of the kindness in your soul. A smile that has no other purpose, than to be smiled. Just stop thinking about yourself. Stop thinking at all, if you can, and do it.

Walk around for the next few days and smile at everyone you pass by. Have zero expectations that they will smile back, or even acknowledge that you did. Smile. And keep on smiling.

If you immediate reaction to this suggestion is one of denial or rejection, ask yourself, "Why?" How is this a difficult thing to do? There are no laws against it. Nobody will call you names, or throw things at you. Nobody will be upset or offended. And even if they are, so what? All you did was smile.

At first, it will likely feel un-natural. I have suggested this exercise to many people and they often report back about how hard it was for them to do it. Often this is because they are afraid of rejection or being an object of derision and scorn. This comes from the past. From old lessons and old rules.

Get past this. It has no place in your new and better future. Just keep doing it and something remarkable will begin to happen. Something wonderful. Something simple and pure and life affirming. They will start to smile back. Not all of them. Some of them can't.

They are too lost. They are so buried under the weight of fear and failure, they cannot even see you. But enough will. More than you expect. And you will feel it. Deep within you. True and lasting pleasure.

This is not just a silly exercise to prove a point. It is actually a form of therapy. When it comes to learning how to deal with our pain and our past, it often helps to explore the option of therapy.

From one-on-one counselling, to group therapy of many descriptions, it is beneficial to seek out as many options as possible.

Often speaking with a therapist, alone or in a group setting, can provide remarkable insights into how best to proceed on your journey. Most of all, it provides a "sounding-board", unbiased and impartial, on which to test your new ideas and explore your new directions. Honestly. Openly. Free of judgement.

CHAPTER 13

Sometimes you need a window, sometimes a mirror

In a Gestalt therapy group I recently attended, there was a sad and bitter elderly man who was raging away in anguish, all the while pounding at a large stack of pillows. The source of all this misery originated over sixty ago when, as a child of seven, he was publically humiliated by his father.

His father had gone out of his way to punish and embarrass him in front of his friends, and the memory of that day had affected every day since. No success he had attained, and he had attained many, was sufficient to balance the shame, and the loss of self-esteem, suffered on that day so long ago.

All of us have memories like this. We carry these slights, real and imagined, around with us for the whole of our lives. Piling new ones on top of the old, until we have so much baggage we need a cart. Worse yet, is the fact that our old fears and failures create new ones of disturbing similarity.

Far too often we cannot help others, or even ourselves, from pushing old buttons. When that occurs, we are right back to where we were when that button was installed. We feel the same shame. The same pain. The same powerlessness. What is worse, is that we feel we are alone. Nobody else could possibly feel like this. This lost. This afraid. This hopeless.

One of the most profound benefits of Gestalt Group Therapy, is that you are able to meet, and come to intimately know, people who are having the same struggles as you. Maybe not the same cause, but certainly the same effect.

You will meet courageous and determined people who not only want to change their lives for the better, but are actively undertaking the actions that will make that possible. You will witness these changes taking place right before your eyes. Often, some of the most revealing personal insights can come through watching another struggle with, and finally overcome, a similar dilemma.

By having created a safe environment, free from judgement and influence, the group allows you to explore and express yourself openly and honestly. Often for the very first time in your life. Without need of shame or regret. Without fear of rejection or reprisal. Without concern for image or status. You can finally be yourself. In search of yourself.

Group Therapy is all about creating that place from which you can begin your journey of self-exploration and then safely return. Gestalt Therapy, in particular, provides you with the opportunity to identify and re-experience the episodes from your past, which have shaped your reactions to, and feelings about, your present.

It becomes possible to isolate and examine those moments of emotional trauma that have shaped the way in which you deal with the world around you, and the way in which you feel about both yourself and others.

This is a deeply personal, often deeply painful, but also extremely freeing experience. Even as an observer. In many strange and wonderful ways, watching others struggle and succeed to overcome the damage done to them, provides both the courage and the encouragement to do so yourself.

Many times, during the sessions I have attended, I have felt myself change as the result of simply witnessing another's experience. Again and again, they would tear themselves open and dig around in their fear and their pain, until they would find the cause of it all.

They would find that one moment, or sadly many, where someone they loved, or someone they trusted, or someone upon whom they depended, had betrayed or abused them. Had shamed or embarrassed them. Had frightened or abandoned them. They would find the buttons. And having found them, they were able to find ways in which to lessen their effect, or, at least, ways in which to better cope when those buttons would, inevitably, be pushed again.

Have you ever had an epiphany? That moment when the proverbial "light bulb" goes on? One minute you are struggling with some deep and painful problem from your past, and the next you can see clearly how it all came to be and, even better, how you can now figure out a way to deal more effectively with it. No?

Well, I have. More than once. I have witnessed this occur again and again in group sessions. People would regress back to the time that caused the trauma. They would re-experience all of the emotions of that time. It was often extremely painful to watch. I would often find myself with tears pouring down my face. Sometimes in sympathy. More often in the empathy of shared experience.

They would weep. They would rage. They would become, for that moment, the small frightened child they had once been. Then, slowly, it would begin to change. They would calm. They would breathe more evenly. The storm of emotions would pass and the light of insight and understanding would start to shine.

They would no longer be the small frightened child crying in the dark. They would, instead, be the intelligent and courageous adult that they are ever more becoming. Each of these experiences was an epiphany. For them. And for many of us who had watched this amazing thing happen. But it doesn't come easily. This is hard. To watch. To do. Especially, to do.

This type of therapy is deeply personal. Success is only possible, if you are willing – and prepared – to literally throw yourself back into the traumas and the terrors of your past. Yes, you can gain great insight, and no small measure of relief, from observing others on their journey, but it is like watching someone drive a car.

No matter how much sense it makes, and how simple it appears, nothing can prepare you for the moment when it is you up there behind the wheel. Especially, if it feels as if you are heading straight for a cliff and the brakes don't seem to be working.

The first time you try it, it is terrifying. Every emotion associated with the original event, comes rushing back in full force. This is perfectly natural. And to be expected. No matter what the experience. However painful. Or frightening. Or shameful. Or debilitating.

The actual experience has long since ended. That moment is over. Whether it happened last Tuesday, or on some other Tuesday half a lifetime ago, it is in the past. What we carry forward into the future, into the lives we now live, is the emotion associated with that experience. It is like a scar from an old wound but, unlike physical scars which seldom hurt anymore, these emotional scars never stop hurting. Until you make them stop.

Emotional pain, especially from past trauma, is a choice. Our suffering does not come from the actual event, it comes from our memory of that event. It comes from the emotional pain we chose to feel on that occasion, and have chosen to hold onto to this day.

The source of the original pain is no longer present. Whatever it was, no matter how horrible it might have been, is over. Yet, you still feel the pain. Why? Because you choose to. And you can choose not to. This is the whole point of any type of therapy.

Learning to make better, or at least different, choices. I spent so much of my "old" life clinging to my pain. At times, it felt like the only thing I actually owned. And it wasn't my fault. No. Never mine. I had so many people I could blame for it.

The horrible bullies at school. My miserable thug of a Grandmother. My disloyal ex-wife and her manipulating mother. They were the ones who had caused my constant unhappiness and my wretched misery. Really. Really?

No, of course not. No matter how it had begun, I was the one who was now responsible for my pain. I was responsible for keeping it, hoarding it, and I was going to have to be the one responsible for getting rid of it. I had to let it go. If I didn't it was going to kill me. I had dodged that bullet once – I had stepped back from the edge – but I knew that I had to get rid of it for good. So, I entered therapy.

The first time I made a real connection with my past trauma, I felt as if I was on fire. I was burning up. Being consumed by all of the fears I still harbored. By all of the failures and regrets I still used to convince myself I was worthless and undeserving of love. Especially my own.

In that instance of complete emotional release, I was able to re-connect with the me I used to be. Before it had all started to go wrong. Before the Tourettes. Before the bullies. Before beatings and the betrayals. I looked at that happy little boy and I thought, "I know him."

I began to understand, as I looked at him, that none of this was his fault. It just happened. It happened around him. It happened to him. I also began to understand, as I looked at who I had become, that what was happening now WAS my fault. I was still allowing the bullies to win. In fact, I had become the biggest bully of all. I was now the one who was stopping me from being . . . me.

As I continued with the therapy, I would return to those situations that had caused me so much pain. I kept going back. I kept experiencing the emotions. I kept feeling the pain. But, each time it would be less emotional, less painful.

I began to understand what had happened – I will never understand why – and I began to see ways I could change. Not change what happened. That is a permanent part of my past. My life. However, while I could not change my past, I could change how I would allow it to make me feel. And I could learn to stop it from influencing the choices I would make in the future.

I began to learn, over time, to recognize what was a valid emotional response to a situation, based on what was actually happening, and what was a "triggered" response to it, based on the overstuffed baggage of my past. I learned to tell the difference between new pain and old. New pain . . . find a way to fix the situation that is causing it. Old pain . . . pat it on the head and send it back to its room.

You need new pain, or at least you can't avoid it, but you do not need old pain. Old pain just stops you from being able to experience anything of true value in your life. It will take every bit of bright color in your life and turn it bleakly gray. Every moment of happiness, of joy, will come with the constant and unrelenting certainty that it is all a lie.

You will never be able to live a full and fulfilling life, an Unstoppable life, unless and until you let go of the old pain that is holding your new life at bay. And yet, letting go of this old pain is often the hardest thing to do.

A few years ago, I had just finished a speaking engagement in San Diego, California. I had a whole in my schedule, a free week to spend on myself, so I rented a shiny blue Mustang convertible and headed up the Pacific Coast Highway. The sun on my face, and the Beach Boys on the stereo, I drove up to Northern California.

My destination was a very special retreat, where only the best and the brightest in the therapeutic community are invited to practice. The leader of my group was one of these extraordinary people. She was an amazing woman, highly skilled and world renowned. What made her choice to help people like us was even more remarkable when I learned that she was slowly falling prey to the ravages of Lou Gehrig's disease.

Amyotrophic Lateral Sclerosis (ALS) is a terrible thing. It is a motor neuron disease that slowly robs you of the ability to swallow, to speak, and eventually to breathe. In spite of the death sentence under which she was living, she had willingly chosen to spend so much of what little time she had left, helping to guide us back to ourselves.

The way the therapy session worked was simple. Each of us would, in turn, take our place on the "hot seat", a chair in the middle of the circle, directly facing the leader. As I said at the beginning, I will not be using anyone's real name, but the first volunteer was a man that I will call Peter.

He was tall and gaunt, with dark melancholy eyes. The sadness came off of him in waves. We could all feel it. He shared with us that he was severely depressed and was living on little more than medication. This had all started a few years earlier, following the death of his partner. A lovely young man, he had brought so much joy into their life together. They were blissfully happy for a time. Unfortunately, that time turned out to be far too short.

This was in the early days of the HIV/AIDS epidemic and few knew how to deal with the devastation it was causing. The available information was limited and the medical treatment available was both expensive and largely inadequate to the task. The young man became ill and, far too soon, fell victim to the disease. Peter was devastated. His whole life had been taken from him as quickly as it had been given.

To make matters worse, the medications that could have prolonged his loving partner's life became available only months after his death. Peter began to feel that he had failed, as both a partner and a professional. As a Registered Nurse, he should have been able to give the love of his life better care. He should have been able to help him to hang on. Until . . .

Severe emotional trauma twists perception. Soon, it was totally Peter's fault that his partner had succumbed to this terrible illness. To have his lover, his life, die in his arms was far too painful for his mind to endure. So, he shut down. He closed himself away in a prison of blame and recrimination. He chose to forfeit his future over the past. A past he had been incapable of controlling. A fight he, and so many millions more, had been incapable of winning.

During the week that I was there, I came to know Peter quite well. Quick-witted and intelligent, he was a delight to be around, but the sadness that followed him always was threatening to consume him. To his credit, he was aware that something had to change. He had to change.

We could all see it. We could all feel it. He had to free himself from the prison his pain had fashioned. He just didn't know how.

Finally, our beloved leader suggested an exercise. She had Peter sit on the floor beside an empty mattress. She had us form a circle around him. Next, she asked him to choose someone from the group. Someone with whom he felt safe. That person was to lay on the mattress and be covered with a sheet.

All of us sat entranced as, almost immediately, Peter was transported back to the moment of his partner's death. It was devastating. The pain and the sorrow flowed out of him without hesitation or restraint. He cried. He howled. He couldn't move. And then he did. He threw himself onto the floor and wept.

His journey toward healing began at that moment. As his sobs diminished, our leader asked Peter to imagine that he was talking to his partner. That he was asking his love for forgiveness. It was deeply moving to share this experience with him.

We were all crying with him, as this imagined conversation took place. Peter said later, that it was as if his partner had really been speaking to him.

Telling him that he would always love him and that Peter had to let go. Let go of the pain and the regret and the guilt. He told Peter that he needed for him to leave the dark and lonely place he was in and move on into one of light and peace.

For therapy to work, you first need to let all of your emotional walls come tumbling down. For this to happen, a group therapy leader has to create a place of safety and support. The group, as a whole, is there to provide that for each and every member of it.

All you, as a participant, is required to do is show up and be willing to force yourself past every barrier of socially acceptable restraint you have ever been taught. Sounds easy, right?

Hardly. What Peter did that day, was one of the bravest things I have ever seen. It also required a level of self-awareness and self-control I thought impossible for anyone to achieve. Certainly someone like me.

And yet, when my turn came, I too was able to make that leap of faith. As did the rest of the group and many more in the sessions I have attended over the ensuing years. This is the power of the therapy. It takes you past your "sticking point". It takes you past societal convention and restrictions. It takes you past the voices in your head. It takes you past your own reluctance to examine old wounds. It breaks you out of the prison to which you have sentenced yourself. Because this is exactly what is necessary for any healing to begin.

You cannot be a spectator to your own therapy. You must be, however hesitant, the one at emotional "ground zero". You have to be right in the middle of it, if you hope to find any way out.

Once Peter had exposed the enormity of his pain and guilt, he was able to begin to build a new and better future free from it. By re-experiencing the trauma of his partner's death, he was finally able to reprocess the information and, essentially, renegotiate – with himself – a new contract for living with the memories of that time.

There are countless stories I could tell you about the "miracles" I have witnessed in Group Therapy. In the next chapter, I will share three more of them with you, but for right now, I want you to take a moment and reflect on Peter's story.

Here was a wonderful young man. Smart, funny, full of life and hopelessly in love. One minute, his life is perfect. The next, it is a living hell. Bleak and barren of all joy and happiness. The love of his life is gone. His own life is meaningless.

Who among us has not felt like this, at one time or another? Perhaps that is exactly how you are feeling right now. Even if it is not quite this bad, there are probably still aspects of your life that cause you to wonder the purpose of it all.

Maybe you believe what Freud said when he wrote, "Life, as we find it, is too hard for us; it brings us too many pains, disappointments and impossible tasks. In order to bear it we cannot dispense with palliative measures. There are perhaps three such measures: powerful deflections, which cause us to make light of our misery; substitutive satisfactions, which diminish it; and intoxicating substances, which make us insensible to it."

If this is where you find yourself, making life bearable instead of truly enjoying the living of it, you might be ready to take the next big step. I assure you that it will be worth it.

CHAPTER 14

You can't hurry love

We live today in a world of instant gratification. Everything we want or need is available to us at a moment's notice. At least that is what we are led to believe.

Once again, we are being told by others what we should do, how we should think and, most of all, the feelings we should have about all of that. We have become so accepting of this, that we don't even question what is happening to us.

If we cannot, for whatever reason, get what we actually need, whatever that may be, we are all too quick to either accept what we can get, or believe them when they tell us that it is not something that we really need, or deserve.

However much this may apply to our material needs, it is even truer when it comes to our emotional needs. If we have an emotion, any emotion, that conflicts or interferes with anyone else, we are more likely to be given a pill to diminish that emotion, than we are to be given the opportunity to openly and honestly express it.

Even if we do not end up being medicated, we are certainly encouraged to "get a hold of" our emotions. This type of conditioning starts in early childhood and it does not take long for it to become the pattern by which we live our lives.

We learn that our emotions are, at best, inconvenient, at worst, inappropriate.

We become convinced that we have no right to feel what we feel. We think that we are somehow failing society by making these unreasonable demands on it. When, in fact, it is our society failing us. We have created an environment of denial that is slowly destroying us and, if we don't fight back, it will soon succeed.

I witnessed the damage this is causing in another group session I attended. Every group therapy leader has his or her own way of helping to direct the experience. This one took a very different "hot seat" approach, from the one I described in the last chapter.

He simply asked us, one at a time, to sit down next to him. He then asked the person on the "hot seat" to take a few deep breaths and relax. He spoke quietly and slowly and helped that person to achieve a mild meditative state.

Once in that state, he asked that person to imagine swallowing a small football shaped object. Having, in his or her mind, done so, the leader then told that person something extraordinary. He said that, what he had given that person to swallow, was not a football at all. It was, instead, a small nuclear device that was going to explode in a few moments.

There was absolutely no way to stop the bomb from exploding. It was timed to the breathing of that person and, after ten breaths, it would explode and destroy every trace of his or her physical existence. All that would be left, would be . . .

The first of us, a rather timid middle-aged man, tried his very best to control his breathing. He even tried holding his breath. In the end, he took his tenth and final breath, and he "exploded". I wish that you could have seen it. It was amazing. He was transformed.

It was as if he had been suddenly freed from bondage. As if the chains that had been holding him down, holding him back, were broken and cast aside. Free from the "thousand shocks that flesh is heir to", as our friend Hamlet so eloquently stated, he could begin to truly open his mind and his heart and feel – for the first time in a long time – genuine unfiltered emotions.

Needless to say, we all clamored to be next. One after another, we all "swallowed" the bomb. The reactions varied, as you might imagine, but none of us were prepared for what happened next.

The person now sitting on the "hot seat" was the sweetest little old lady you had ever seen. I will call her Molly. The quintessential storybook "Granny", she had won all our hearts with her kindness and gentle support. She had always been the first one to hand a tissue or give a hug to each of us, as we recovered from the "bomb". Now it was her turn. But first, I must give you a little of her story.

Molly had recently suffered a massive heart attack. As traumatic as that was, her real problem was with the treatment she had received at the hands of the EMTs. By the time they had arrived, she had already begun to fail. She was fading in and out of consciousness, so they went right to work.

First they gave her an injection to prevent any uncontrollable movement. Then, they brought out the paddles. You have all seen this on television. It is called a defibrillator and it is, essentially, the same idea as using a car battery to jump-start your engine. It fires jolts of electricity, between 200 and 1000 volts, to try and stabilize the rhythm of a heart in cardiac arrest.

They fired the paddles. Once. Then again. And again. By the fifth time they shocked her, Molly said that it felt as if her teeth were smoking. However, as horrible as this was, what bothered her most, was their seeming indifference. All through this horrible experience, the EMTs completely ignored her as a person. They were just dealing with her body. It went so far, as to them discussing last night's football game between administering these painful electric shocks.

The more she talked about the experience, the more she relived it, the angrier she became. We sat astonished, as this dear sweet woman became the Linda Blair character from the "The Exorcist". All that was missing, was the pea soup.

"You fucking bastard assholes! I fucking hate you! I want to rip your balls off! I want to stick fucking knives in your eyes!"

It all came pouring out of her. Her frustration. Her anger. Her pain. She relived every moment of that horrible day and we lived it with her. It, quite frankly, scared the crap out of most of us. Her anger was a living thing. A terrifying creature that was loose and tearing about the room. A creature that had been living inside this wonderful woman and had been eating her up inside for all this time.

The leader was amazing. He slowly and calmly brought her back, out of the depths of her anguish and back to the safety of the group. He asked her, as she began to quieten, "What do you need to say to these EMTs?" In a surprisingly peaceful voice, she said, "All I wanted was for you to tell me what was happening. To say, "You're having a heart attack. We want to save your life. We are so sorry, but what we are going to do will hurt you. It will hurt, but it will save your life. Please forgive us, but we really need to do this if we are to save you".

All I wanted was for you to look into my eyes, maybe touch my face, and tell me what was happening."

But they had not done that. They focused on the "problem", not the person with the problem. This has happened to all of us, maybe not to the extreme way it happened to Molly, but all of us have been in a situation that has had lasting consequences. Our needs were ignored, or pushed aside, in the desire to expedite a situation. Maybe once. Maybe often.

Whatever it was, it happened. And it had an effect. It still does. It is a part of our experience. But, it can get even worse. If it happens enough, we will start to do it to ourselves. We won't wait for someone else to do it. We will shut it down. Lock it away. Turn off the emotion at the source. We will do it. And the cost is enormous.

I chose to go last, on that day. The leader went through the whole "swallow the football" speech and I grabbed it with both hands. I didn't wait for the clock to tick down. I huffed and puffed and counted the ten deep breaths and then it happened. I exploded. One moment I am there, sitting in that chair, and the next, I am free of my body and happily floating in the air. Way above my body. High above my life.

I was no longer Stuart. I wasn't even human, at that point. I just felt like energy. And it was wonderful. I was completely at ease. For the first time in a very long time. I wasn't angry. I wasn't depressed. There was no reason to hide. There was nothing to fear. I was happy.

No, I was more than happy. I was blissfully content. No negative emotions existed in this beautiful place. Everything had gone from darkness to light. From earthbound heaviness to floating weightless in space. I was free. Free to be me. Free not to care if I was.

It was almost as if I could touch the infinite. No one knows, least of all me, what God is. I have spent most of my life looking for answers to questions I didn't even understand.

At that moment, neither the questions nor the answers mattered. All that mattered was to be in that moment. I floated above my life. I could see it laid out below me. The whole of my life was there, within view but out of reach. I was at peace. Then I heard the leader ask, "Where are you?" I told him. Then he said, "Take me to that place where you do not want to go."

Instantly, I came crashing down into complete darkness. Into a Hell of my own making. Screaming and crying and spewing out a torrent of anger and frustration and long repressed emotions.

One moment I am peacefully floating in the heavens, the next I am writhing on the floor. Looking for all the world as if I had just been Tasered. Every repressed thought and emotion, every memory, was being re-experienced. It was totally out of control.

The negative feelings that had all been so carefully packed away, came bursting out. It was like an explosion of pain. There was no time for me to process any of them, let alone them all. I felt like I was standing in front of a flame-thrower and it was aimed at me.

I could not get out of the way and I certainly could not stop it. And, strangely, I didn't want to. Somewhere inside, I knew that it was time.

The leader said, "Look down. What do you see?" I didn't know quite how to express it. As I looked down, I saw my life laid out like a river, flowing from horizon to horizon. I could see it, much like a sepia toned photograph from an old scrap book, faded and hazy.

It was all there and I could stop and look at any part of that river. Instantly, the memories of that point in time would come to me. Every thought. Every emotion. Every moment was mine to re-explore. To re-experience.

Then, the leader asked me to do something. Something I had always been dreading. He asked me to attend my own funeral. I felt myself in the coffin. I felt myself being lowered into the ground. "Look up", he said, "tell me what you see."

I told him that I was surrounded by all of the bullies who had terrorized me so at school. "What are they saying?" he asked. "What are they doing?"

I struggled to answer him. I almost couldn't speak. I could not believe what I was seeing. What I was hearing. They were all crying. They were all saying the same thing. "We are so very sorry. For bullying you. For hurting you. We didn't know. We were just children, we didn't understand. Please forgive us."

I was on the floor, hunched over, shaking, bathed in sweat. I was crying. Snot was dripping from my nose.

And then a small voice forced its way from deep inside me. The voice of the child I had never been allowed to be. By fate or by circumstance. This small voice spoke for the first time. It said, "Can I go play now?"

I remember looking up and seeing everyone in the group, gathered around me, with tears in their eyes. Such is the power of the group experience. It forces you to look at your deepest fears. At your most repressed memories. At all your failures and all your faults.

But it does not ask you to do this alone. One of the greatest benefits of the group therapy experience, is that it reminds you that you are never alone in your suffering. All around you, others are suffering too. Struggling just as hard as you, to find their true potential.

The damage done to our young and tender souls can cause us all to turn ever inward, until we become so blinded by the pain of these memories that we are unaware that the life we are so desperately seeking is passing silently by. This angry, self-defeating, narcissism shuts us off from the world of opportunities around us. Around you.

The world in which you live, is smaller than the world in which you deserve to live. The only way to find this space, is to clean house. That is what makes Group Therapy, any therapy, so important. And so beneficial.

As you start to strip away the layers of painful memories and get at the causes, and the effects, of the actions of others, in your past, and your own, today, you begin to understand something profound. You begin to understand that everything you need to have this new and wonderful life, everything that will take you to it, is already there inside you.

Your strength is hidden in your weakness. Your courage is hidden in your fear. Your solutions are hidden away under your problems.

For the longest time, I did not know this. If someone had told me what I just told you, I would have said he or she was crazy. I was weak, not strong. I was fearful, not brave. And worst of all, there were no solutions to the problems I had. I truly believed that. I probably still would, if it had not been for that horrible/beautiful day.

Yes, it was that day when I found myself standing on my balcony, ready to step over the edge that finally forced me to be open to the, very slight, possibility that I did not actually have a clue. I simply did not know how to live a life that was tolerable, let alone Unstoppable.

I went, all too willingly, from one disappointment to another. Storing them up. Hiding them away. Burying myself in my misery. It had to end. So, I was going to die. Kill myself. That would be the end I was searching for.

One of the more tragic aspects of suicide, is that it does not actually give you the answers you are seeking. It just ends the conversation. And that is the exact opposite of what you truly need. You need more conversations. With yourself. Good or bad.

That is one of the best things about therapy, in that it lets you get up close and personal with both your angels and your demons. It will answer questions you never even thought to ask.

One last painful personal story and then we can move on. I was participating in another group therapy session one day and I was feeling more stressed than usual. It was coming close to my turn and I excused myself to go to the washroom. I was feeling quite ill. I don't know about you, but I hate throwing up. I will do just about anything to avoid it.

What I did not realize, at the time, was the mind hates vomiting just as much as does the body. My mind simply did not want to puke all of my pain out on the floor. Anyway, I washed my face and headed back into the room.

I came back with an attitude. I walked up to the leader and said, "Okay. You told us that when we sit on the hot seat, we should get right to the point. Well, I am sitting here . . . let's get on with it." I will never forget the way she smiled at me.

She told me to choose a cast of characters from the group. These were the people who would help me with my experience. They would be the "actors" in the play of my life. I chose carefully. The pretty young blond would be my ex-wife. The sour faced, grumpy looking middle-aged woman would be my ex-mother-in-law. There were a couple of other people in minor roles, but I was very deliberate in my choice of a safe person.

The young woman I selected was a very shy and timid person. She was almost always shaking. It was easy to understand why. She had grown up in the Philippines, with an alcoholic father who would, without fail, physically abuse at least one member of her family every night. Maybe I thought that this exercise would help her to be able to take this journey herself. Maybe I just wanted someone who was as scared as I was. Anyway, the cast assembled, we began.

And I hit the ground running. It was as if I had stripped myself naked in front of them. I let it all hang out. Every bit of anger and resentment against my ex and her mother, especially her mother, came gushing forth. It boiled up in me and poured out over the floor.

All of the bitterness. All of the recrimination. All of the rejection. All of the hatred. I screamed at the woman playing my ex-wife's mother. I reviled her without restraint. I hurled all of my pain in her face. I accused her of treachery and deceit. I told what I wanted to do to her, in no uncertain terms.

Hannibal Lecter would have been proud of the torture I told her I wished to inflict upon her. I had lit my world on fire and I was reaching for more fuel.

For almost fifteen minutes, I raged away. This must sound horrific to you, and in many ways it was, but I believe that there is something hidden deep inside all of us that has the potential to erupt like this. So many of us walk around with these unresolved issues that just continue to fester away inside us, until the day they finally force their way out.

Group Therapy gives you a safe and controlled environment in which to allow, even encourage, this to happen. There is also something very important about having the other people there. Sure, it can be a little embarrassing at first, but there is something so validating about having witnesses to the experience. They are there to watch the old pain leave and the new power take its place.

Suddenly, the leader shouted over my ranting, "You're not letting me in." Instantly, I responded, "Fuck you! Don't you get it? You can't have him. He is mine."

As soon as I said this, I realized what was happening. In that moment, I felt as if I was living in a cold, dark, wet cave and I could not get out. I could see a monster guarding the entrance to the cave. A large dark mass of anger and resentment blocking any light from entering and me from leaving.

This was the prison I had created for myself and my negative emotions were the chains that were keeping me held fast in this nightmare. I felt completely powerless. I was, once again, small and afraid. Surrounded by monsters.

"What don't you understand? I protect him. I am the only thing keeping him alive. Without me, he would be destroyed." The monster screamed. From seemingly off in the distance, I heard the group leader ask a question. "This is not worth it", he said. "Do you want to let this go?"

From the back of the cave, I cried out, "Yes."

It was the only thing I could say. I had finally come to the realization of the all too bitter truth. I had put myself into this place. I had created this prison. I had created the monster. I was responsible for this and I could see what I had become because of it. I was wasting away. I was the classic dungeon victim.

Scrawny and emaciated. Dirty and ragged. Not to the seeing eye, of course, but deep within. I had become a character from a Defoe novel. I was the Prisoner of Zenda. I had been cast into a prison of pain, while an imposter who looked like me lived the shadow that was my life. And I had done it to myself.

The leader's eyes never left mine. "If you want to live free of this, get down on your hands and knees." So, I did. And, when I did, it all changed. The anger became sorrow. As my knees hit the floor, all of the pain and frustration that had been carefully hidden away after all of the years of being bullied and beaten, ridiculed and rejected, broke free and came washing over me. My anger could no longer contain it.

The leader asked the others to come forward and surround me. But, they had ceased to be the demons of my past. They had become my angels. They held me as I fell forward. They picked me up and supported me as I cried. They helped me to my feet and stayed with me, by my side.

The young woman I had chosen to be my "safe person" put her head on my shoulder. "Thank you", she whispered. "I have never seen anyone get so angry before and not hurt anyone else." She had stopped shaking.

"Remember this moment', the leader said. "All of us here understand your pain. How much your ex-wife and her mother hurt you. Maybe, in time, you will be able to forgive them, but first you must forgive yourself. None of this was ever your fault."

During this exercise, the leader invited me to accept Grace into my life. I asked her what "Grace" was, as I was unaware of the meaning in this context. She shared with me and the group that, when we no longer have the capability to forgive ourselves, we need to reach outside of ourselves and connect to a higher power.

Call it whatever you want – God, or collective consciousness, or Universal Energy - but whatever you call it, it allows us to remove ourselves from the equation and become objective and thereby achieve the state of awareness and forgiveness that has been alluding us.

I wish that I could tell you that it happened instantly. That in that one moment, I was able to overcome all that had happened. It wasn't that easy. It wasn't that fast. But it did happen. Eventually. I was able to see things as they really were and not the overly good, or overly bad, versions that existed only in my mind. I could finally see the truth.

The bullies of my youth were only stupid children, completely unaware of the damage they were causing. My Grandmother was a bitter and disappointed old woman, so beaten down by her own life she could only find some release through beating another. My ex-wife was a victim of her own fantasies.

She had wanted nothing more than a fairy tale romance with a dashing prince. Unfortunately, the prince she chose had a few problems she couldn't handle. She was frightened and, in her fear, she ran away.

Even her mother had her reasons. Left alone, following the death of her husband, she struggled to raise her daughters as best she could. Her own fears of this happening to her girls, brought her to the edge of reason and she instilled that same fear into her children.

Each and every person who has ever harmed me in any way has had a reason for it. The reasons may not be good ones, but reasons there were. I may never understand them. I don't even try anymore.

Whatever the reasons might have been, I no longer care. I refuse to let them affect me now. I will not any longer deny myself the pleasures of the present, and future, because I am clinging to the pain of the past.

I deserve to be happy. I deserve to be loved. I deserve to have days filled with joy and nights filled with peace. I deserve it. And so do you.

CHAPTER 15

Beyond here be dragons

When ancient cartographers would draw their maps, they would illustrate the world as it was known to them. When they reached the limit of their knowledge, they would simply fill in the space around the edges with the admonition: Beyond Here Be Dragons.

Entering into therapy, of any type, can often seem the same. You know that you want to change. Your life. Or, at least, how you feel about your life. You want to begin to be the person you know you should have always been. You are just not entirely sure what that means. You have identified a place from which to start, you just don't know where it will all end.

Therapy can only help you so much with that. It cannot "tell" you who you are going to be. It can only help you to understand who you are and how you got to be that way. Examining the past. Vividly re-experiencing those pivotal moments in your history. Exorcizing the demons that have plagued you for so long. These will all enable you to better understand how you became the person you are.

Therapy will help you to clarify the reasons why you do, think and feel the way you do. It will not, however, give you any idea – at all – of how to become more/better/different. Those choices are entirely up to you. Deciding the person you want to become is your job. It actually always has been. You just didn't know that. Maybe you thought your life path would be something that you would be given. Maybe you didn't think about it at all.

This is not, in any way, unusual. Our society was founded on a small number of people, telling a large number of people what to do, how to think, who to be. This is the same dynamic in a nuclear family, as it is in a Nuclear Power. Governments control the populous. Parents control children. The only difference, is that you don't get to elect your parents. And you can't vote them out of office, if they are doing a bad job. You cannot actually "fire" your parents. You can, however, quit.

This may well have been the most controversial statement I will make in this entire book. The very idea that you can, somehow, quit your parents seems both unreasonable and unthinkable to most people. And yet, it may be exactly what you need to do. But why?

First of all, I am not going to say that your parents were horrible people. I know that there are parents out there for whom this would definitely apply, but, for the most part, parents are just people with kids. Some good. Some better. Some, unfortunately, not.

Being a parent is an enormous responsibility. And it is a job that comes with absolutely no clear cut set of instructions. There is no training available on how to be a good parent, other than what they learned from their own.

Sometimes, they were great parents. Understanding. Supportive. Encouraging. Kind. And, most of all, loving. Sometimes, they just weren't. Often, forces beyond themselves made it difficult, if not downright impossible for them to be the perfect parents. At least, the perfect parents for you.

My darling wife Doris, is a classic example of this.

Although she was born in Canada, her parents had come from the Canton region of China. Struggling to cope with a new and often confusing language, they only spoke Chinese at home.

As a consequence, by the time Doris started school she was perfectly fluent in her parent's language. Unfortunately, she couldn't speak a word of English. Try to imagine the confusion she felt. The frustration. The embarrassment. The shame.

Had her parents meant for her to feel this way? Of course they hadn't. Had they caused it? Of course they had. The limitations in themselves had created a limitation in their child. Their unwillingness to change, to adapt, to accept their new situation, had caused a real and lasting problem for their daughter.

Now she was forced to struggle past both a language barrier, that should have never existed, and a sense of self-consciousness and lessened self-esteem, at a critical point in any young child's life.

Unfortunately, that was not the only issue. Cultural differences were also a problem. In spite of the many beautiful qualities that make up the Asian culture, there are also elements of it that can be difficult to integrate into those of the west. The role of women in the family, for example.

Doris was raised to accept that men were superior. They always came first. Women came second, if at all. Formal education was, for a girl, simply not a priority. Learning to be a quiet, obedient, self-effacing, wife, however, was. And any resistance to that, would not be tolerated. Forget about refusing to do something. Even questioning why she should have to, would result in harsh scolding. Or worse.

Many of the young girls, growing up under these conditions, succumb to the indoctrination. They become their mothers. And, once mothers themselves, go on to raise their daughters in the same way. Not, however, my wonderful, strong, independent wife. She chose a different path.

At the age of eighteen, she "quit". Her parents may well have thought that they were still the management, but Doris stopped being their employee. She moved out. She began working. She sought out more and better education. She made more and better choices. And the choices she made, were her own.

Were they always the right ones? No. Everybody makes mistakes. Questionable hairstyles. Jobs that didn't work out. A marriage that failed. Two steps forward, one step back. But she kept moving. She kept making choices. I am, and will always be, so very proud and grateful that one of those choices, was me.

Today, the love of my life is a dynamic and accomplished woman. She has a challenging and rewarding career. She has raised two children of her own. Strong and independent and as free from the shadows of the past as possible. She is both a killer tennis player and the kindest person I have ever known.

Together we navigate this world, and this life, searching for every moment of joy we can possess. I can only hope that I leave this world first, for I cannot bear the thought of my life without her. Any more than I can bear the thought that I almost never knew her.

Had we both chosen to remain the prisoners of our former lives, we would have never met. Had we never made the choice to choose, we would not be here now.

We would be trapped in some lesser life, not even daring to dream that such joy, such happiness, such love could ever be ours.

Now, I am not saying that her parents would not have wanted Doris to be happy. They just wanted it to be on their terms. Under their rules.

This is something that all parents, however unwittingly, do to their children. Along with the rules of civil behavior – all of the "yes, please" and "no, thank you" and "anything you say, sir" – parents also instill an overwhelming array of fears and prejudices and assumptions and doubt. The rules are often contradictory, but they are never to be questioned. And they are always to be followed. No matter what.

What? How does that make any sense? Clearly, it doesn't. And, what makes it worse, is they don't even know that they are doing it. They unknowingly, but with great enthusiasm, pass on the failures of the past. And then wonder why their children continue to fail.

Almost everybody understands that the child of an abuser, often becomes one. Alcoholic parents raise alcoholic children. We get this. What we don't seem to get, is that the same is true for just about every other trait.

Fearful parents raise children who live in fear. Apathetic parents raise children who care about little, if anything. Violent parents raise children who fight the world. And prejudiced parents raise children who hate it. The only way to break this cycle, is to break this cycle. Be the change you are waiting for. Become someone new. Someone different.

This is exactly where I found myself so many years ago. I had broken the barriers in my mind and freed the little boy I used to be.

Now I had a responsibility to him. I had become the parent to myself. Now what? First, I had to become brutally, painfully, honest with myself. What in my life worked? What didn't? Which rules applied to my new life? Which didn't? What should I choose? What could I choose?

Eventually, I learned that those choices made free from the bias and beliefs of others worked. The ones made out of the conflict and confusion of the past didn't. Was this easy? Not even a little bit.

It wasn't for me and it won't be for you. Each step you take on this journey will feel as if you are walking on eggs. Or, worse yet, broken glass. Every time you try something new, you will hear the chorus of negative voices from your past crying out in dismay.

Every time that you make a new rule for yourself, you will hear the vociferous arguments being put forward by the ones who first made the rules you are about to break. Ignore these voices. Not one of them is yours.

At least it shouldn't be. Be very careful here. Do not allow the fear and insecurity to discourage or dissuade you from taking chances. From making changes. From writing your own rules. You will be tempted. Sorely tempted. It will seem far easier to give up. Go back to the way you were. To stop trying new and frightening things. But, not only will you regret it, it is now virtually impossible for you to do so.

Have you ever heard of the term, "Death by GPS"? This is not a joke. The number of people who have blindly followed their car's navigation device, or even their cellphone, to an untimely demise is staggering. They have followed their SatNav into deserts. Or lakes. Or off cliffs. How could anybody be that stupid? Is it stupidity? Isn't it what we have always been taught? Trust those who know better.

They will steer you in the right direction. And they will. If where you want to go is out in the middle of nowhere. Lost and alone.

Obviously, this doesn't happen all the time. I routinely use my GPS and it, more often than not, will get me where I want to go. Mine hasn't tried to kill me. Yet!

But this does serve as a fairly appropriate analogy. When you are making choices, any choices, the results are directly dependent on two things. The quality of the information you are using to assist in the decision making. And your ability to understand, or even recognize, the validity of it to the current situation.

In an earlier chapter, I wrote about Selective Perception and Cognitive Dissonance. Remember? Well, just in case you don't, I will remind you of what those things mean and how they affect your life. I won't go into the long explanation this time. All I will do, is give you a new name for them. Let's call it what it is. A Blind Spot. We all have them. We all suffer from them. Don't believe me? Try this.

Hold this book in one hand. Okay, now take your other hand and put it in front of your eyes. Can you still see the book? Can you read it? No. Whatever information that exists here, is now lost to you. All you can see is your hand. But even that isn't true. Actually, all you can see is part of your hand. If you move that hand too close to your face, all you will be able to see is . . . nothing. You will be in darkness. And who did this? You did.

The same thing is true, when we try to make choices based on, or around, our blind spots. Where do these blind spots come from? They come from our past. These are the "gifts" we have been given by others. The rules and regulations that were taught to us.

To be fair, some of these rules will keep you alive and healthy. Look both ways before you cross the street. Never ever smoke in bed. Don't spit into the wind. Never eat the yellow snow. Good rules, all of them. And there are more. There are, however, some terrible rules out there. One of the worst is this one: Don't trust anything new.

How many times have you heard someone say, "Don't fix it if it ain't broken"? Hundreds? Thousands? Maybe you even say it yourself. Well, I have some news for you. It is broken. It is always broken. It always has been. And it always will be.

I don't even care what "it" is, there is probably a better, safer, cheaper, more effective way to do just about everything. Including, live your life. So, what is stopping you?

BLIND SPOTS. Everywhere you look. Don't believe me? Try this. Try and remember the last time you were offered an opportunity to do something new. Did you just go ahead and do it? Or, did you stop and instantly think of all the things that could go wrong and all the reasons why you would be better off to just let the opportunity pass?

Now, I am not suggesting that you should do, or try, every new thing that comes along. What I am suggesting is that you should be completely honest in your reasons for either of the following choices. Do it. Don't do it.

You are absolutely allowed to not like, or not enjoy, anything. You don't have to try everything. Just ask yourself, "Why?" Were you simply disinterested, or were you afraid. Was there any voice, other than your own, telling you to avoid this opportunity?

I sometimes think that I am far luckier than the average person. The "normal" person. My grab-bag of mental issues has one very interesting consequence. My mind's natural tendency is to bounce around like a crazed pinball, so I have had to learn to focus intently on whatever it is that I am trying to do. Once I have set my mind to something, it becomes the total focus of my concentration.

In the past, this was often a problem. Because most of my decisions were based on bad intel, I would focus on the negatives. I would filter every new experience through the failures of the old. In spite of this, I would relentlessly keep trying to move forward. Often, however, I had no idea where "forward' was going to take me.

A lot of people talk about "freedom". How much they want it. How much they need it. How much they deserve it. And most of them can't even tell you what it is. This is because freedom is not actually "a" thing. It is two very separate and distinctly different things.

There is Freedom From. From pain. From suffering. From a bad job. From a worse marriage. This is the freedom we all know and think about. It is the freedom most of us seek when we purchase those lottery tickets. If we can only hold out until we win the lottery, then we can leave this place . . . this job . . . this life . . . and be happy.

Sadly, this seldom happens. Even if you do win. Often lottery winners have not gone on to have wonderful lives. In fact, many of them end up back in the poverty and despair from which they came. Why? Simple. Most of those who ended up back where they started, did so because they had no idea of where they wanted to go. They just knew that they wanted to get away from where they were.

That was their wish. Unfortunately, they didn't need yet another "wish". What they needed was a plan.

The other type of freedom, is Freedom For. This is the freedom that will change your life for the better. This is the freedom that replaces wishes with plans. This is the freedom that can and will truly change your life. A life filled with choices. A life filled with accomplishments. A life filled with satisfaction. A, once and for all, Unstoppable life.

How you get there is entirely up to you. It will be different for every person who is reading this book. It is not up to me to tell you what it should be, but I can help you to make the right choice. For me, it was quite easy. I knew, almost immediately, what I wanted to do. From the moment I had broken free from the chains of my past and emerged from the prison of my pain, I knew that I wanted to help others.

At first, I just wanted to help them be better at their jobs. I made it my job. That is why I became a public speaker. In my "old life", I had often been asked, by friends and colleagues, clients and suppliers, even total strangers, how it was that someone like me – twitchy old weirdo me – could have achieved any success at all, let alone the success I had achieved.

So, I knew that maybe I had some answers that others were seeking. Initially, I would make a joke about it. I was still self-conscious and convinced that they were only looking for an opportunity to insult or ridicule me. Remember, this was in my old life. I was still the old me.

After I had begun to take control of my life – my new life – I began to take these questions more seriously. To the point of making the answering of these questions my career. I now have hundreds of clients, in dozens of industries, who rely on me to provide the information and insight that will help their people become better at doing their jobs. I love these people. And I love my job. But it still was not enough.

Sure, I was helping people to be better workers, but was I helping them to be better people? I struggled with this question for quite some time. Slowly, I began to change the nature of my presentations. I still focused on the tangibles, the work that needed to be done, but I also began to include the more esoteric aspects of working and living more effectively.

Those stories and ideas and awareness that I have been sharing with you in this book. Did I lose clients because of this? No. I have, from the very first, witnessed this improve the relationships with my existing clients, and it has enabled me to go on to gain many more. Often through direct referral from my current clients and their staff.

I do not say this to be boastful. I admit it, I am successful. I make no apologies for having built the life I am living. I am proud of it. As the accident victim said to the ambulance attendant, when he was asked if he was comfortable, "I make a good living."

The reason I tell you this, and every other story in this book, is to encourage you. Get out there. Make the changes you need to make. For every person who opposes these changes, there will be countless others who will embrace them. And you. There is something amazing that happens when you become the "hero" in your own life. You often become the hero in the lives of those you touch along the way.

Just as the ancient mariners of old who, so determined to explore and conquer new worlds, would ignore the warning, "Beyond here be dragons".

You must venture forth into uncharted waters and face the mighty forces of nature. You must be prepared to overcome the many obstacles. You must be ready to face the dragons.

When you do, you will be surprised by the results. You will become an inspiration. You will become a reason to hope. A reason to try. You will become the architect of your own life and the example for those who seek to do the same.

In addition, you will become happier. More confident. More capable. You will become calmer. More peaceful. More tolerant. More understanding. You will become a better parent. And partner. A better student. And teacher. A better friend.

Most of all, you will become, and you will remain, the only thing that really matters in this life. You will become UNSTOPPABLE.

CHAPTER 16

There are no guarantees

A few years back, I was standing on the deck of a small cruise ship, somewhere off the Yasawa Islands of Fiji, when my lovely wife Doris came up to me and said, "I love being your wife." I was understandably thrilled, but I decided to play around with her, so I asked, "Why?"

She looked at me for a moment and smiled. "Well", she said, "for all the obvious reasons, I suppose, but also because of this. We are on this wonderful cruise. We are having a fabulous time. And we don't even have to pay for it, because you are working."

After we had finished laughing about what she had said, I started to think about how much my life had changed. Here I was living a life I could never have hoped for. Never even imagined. I was working for myself. Doing something I truly enjoyed. I was making a good living. I was married to the love of my life. I was writing my own rules. My life was as close to perfect as I could have ever wished for it to be.

The reason I was on board, was that I was shooting social network videos for a client. I was interviewing the passengers about their cruise and how much they were enjoying the experience. Things were going great. We were ahead of schedule. The responses had been even better than expected. We had tons of footage. And, the best part, tomorrow was a day off. But, not just an ordinary day off.

The cruise was scheduled to anchor of the coast of a beautiful little island that just happened to be where the movie "The Blue Lagoon" had been filmed. It was one of the most beautiful places I had ever seen on film and now I was actually going to see it for real.

Even better was the fact that we were going to be able to go diving. I had been diving for about ten years, at this point, in some of the most exotic locations on this planet. I was a qualified and experienced diver. I had always felt perfectly safe in the water. And I was looking forward to this experience, more that I can express.

At first, it was everything I had hoped. More. To even try and describe what I was seeing, let alone how I was feeling, would be impossible. Words are inadequate. It was wonderful. And then it wasn't. I began to have trouble breathing.

At first I thought it was a problem with the equipment, but everything checked out. I could not figure out what was happening. Whatever it was, it was getting worse. It was getting harder and harder to breath.

I struggled to the surface. When I took off my mask and removed the diving regulator from my mouth, I started to spew pink froth. They immediately rushed me back to the ship. By then, I was close to passing out. They put me back in our cabin and did the best they could to help me.

The medical facilities they had were very basic and there was not much that they could do. The next couple of days were horrible. I was in pain and I was terrified. I did not know what was happening to me.

As soon as we landed back in Canada, I went to see my doctor who immediately called an ambulance and I was rushed to the hospital.

One minute, I am swimming in the warm luxurious waters of the South Pacific. The next, I am lying on a cold slab of an examination table, being told that I had suffered a massive heart attack and that my heart had become dangerously enlarged.

I will never forget the cardiac specialist standing over the table and telling me that I needed immediate open heart surgery. The diagnosis was frightening enough, but what made it worse was the way he said it. For all the emotion he showed, he might as well having been telling me I needed to change the oil in my car.

What was worse, was that the surgery might not work. I could die at any moment. I was going to need a heart transplant. And then he turned to Doris and asked if I had a will. Just in case. I will never forget the look on her face. My beautiful wife, who had only days before been telling me how much she enjoyed our life together, was now being told to get ready to face a life alone. She instantly burst into tears.

This may sound odd to you. Maybe even terrible. But, in spite of the "death sentence" I had just been handed, what was going through my mind, as I watched my dear wife sobbing her eyes out, was "Wow. What do you know? She really does love me." I was amazed. I had been convinced that I was unloved – unlovable – for so much of my life, it stunned me to see just how much she did love me. It touched me to the very depths of my poor badly damaged heart.

At that moment, I knew that I was not going to die. I simply had too much to do. I still had so much that I needed to accomplish. I had made up my mind. I wasn't dying. I knew it. All I had to do now, was convince the doctor. Not an easy thing to do. Talk about the irresistible force meeting the immovable object.

I don't really blame them. I mean, all I was to them was the dying guy. What the hell did I know about it? They were the experts. The next day another surgeon said to me, "We have put you through all the tests and we have checked all the numbers. Your heart is twice the size it should be and so weak it could go at any minute. We don't even know why you are still alive, let alone awake and arguing with us."

So, they put me on the transplant list and sent me home. Over the next six weeks, I was seen by doctor after doctor and they all had the same advice. Kiss your loved ones "Goodbye" and get ready for the end.

That was tough to take, but what made it worse, was the casual disregard they had for me as a person. I was just another "case" to them. At best a curiosity, because I was still alive, but not really a still living, still breathing human being. I was merely a dead guy who didn't know it yet. Who wouldn't accept the inevitable.

Then I met the man who saved my life. His name is Saul Isserow. A South African transplant to Canada, he looked at me. I mean actually looked . . . at me . . . and said, "Stewie, my boy. Your heart is a little horrible. But, don't you worry, mate, I am going to make it right as rain. No worries." And he did.

Over the next few months, he was able to identify the real problem – a relatively rare but easy to address pacing issue – and the solution for it. A Pacemaker was installed and, over time, my heart reduced in size back to normal. Today, I am as healthy as I have ever been. Maybe more so. I went from climbing weakly into bed each night, thinking that this night could be my last, to starting each new day with an hour long hike.

As grateful as I am to Dr. Isserow and his amazing team, for saving my life, I am equally grateful for the near loss of it. Coming that close to death made me more aware of life than I have ever been.

Facing death made me even more determined to face life. As messy and miserable as it might be, from time to time, it is also an incredible gift. Best of all, it is a gift you get to share. Must share.

I know, for an absolute fact, that each of you will come to some point in your life when you are faced with the realization that you only have a finite amount of time on this earth. It could be anything that causes this. A car accident where you narrowly escape death. The sickness of your child. It could even be an experience such as mine.

Whatever it is, it will open your eyes to what is truly important. It will clear away the cobwebs of doubt and the clouds of confusion that have so obscured your vision for so long and you will be able to finally see the reality of your life. And the need to live it to its fullest.

Fear and doubt and regret are replaced with courage and clarity and acceptance. Most of all, you will feel an enormous sense of gratitude. For this life of yours. With all of its bumps and bruises. All of its warts and scars.

From this terrible moment of fear, comes a wonderful place of peace. It is a place to which you can return at any time. Do you remember those places of safety you probably created as a child? A place where you could hide from all of those imaginary monsters.

Maybe it was a tent made from blankets, or a fort made of pillows. It might have been nothing more than an empty cardboard box, but it was your safe place. It was a place you could go to hide away from the world. If only for a moment. Almost every child has one.

As adults, however, we are not supposed to hide inside a cardboard box, or pillow fort, when the world gets to be too much for us. We are expected to stand up and take what is coming at us. To us.

We are not supposed to be afraid, even though the world is likely to be far scarier now than it was when we were children. Far too often now, the monsters are real. Debt. Divorce. Disease. Disappointment. Our lives are filled with these monsters and we no longer have a safe place to hide away for a moment and just chill out. Or do we?

What I am about to share with you was a core breakthrough for me. It came to me as a direct consequence of the near death situation caused by my seriously damaged heart. In that moment of learning that I was about to die, I also learned that my life had meaning. It had value. It was worth so much more than I could have ever believed.

If I had actually died, at that moment, I would still have been grateful for the life I had lived. All of the struggles. All of the successes. All of the pain. All of the joy. I was appreciative, beyond measure, for everything that had gone into my life. And everything that had come out of it. I was at peace. Finally and honestly. At peace.

Of course, I didn't die. I know that one day I will and I will be ready for it. Certainly, it will come too soon. It always does. But I will be so very appreciative for each and every day I will have before then. I will never lose that sense of boundless gratitude for the life I have enjoyed. The life I created for myself. This Unstoppable life.

Sure, there are times when I need to be reminded. Life can get in the way of the best of intentions, but I have discovered a way to get back to this place of gratitude and acceptance. Pretty much any time I want. And I can teach it to you. But first, you have to die.

Okay, you don't have to actually die. You just have to imagine that you are. As odd as this might sound, it is easy to do. And it is worth it.

First, you need to find someplace quiet. Someplace where you will not be disturbed. If you have other people in your home, especially tiny ones, let them know that you need a little time to yourself. Be subtle about it. Just put up a big sign on the door that reads, "Do not disturb, under pain of death . . . or broccoli."

Close the door. Turn off the lights. Lie down. On a couch. On a bed. On the floor. It doesn't matter. Just lie down. Okay, take a really deep breath. Suck in as much air as you can. Fill your lungs. Now empty them. Exhale. Completely. Slowly blow all of that air out. Once you are empty, tell yourself, "I am not going to breathe." And don't.

At first, for a moment or two, it will be easy. Pretty soon, however, your body will begin to disagree with what you are doing. It will want to breathe. Tell it, "No!" Your body will not want to hear that. It will begin to fight back. Your anxiety level will start to rise. Your heart will start to pound. Every instinct in your body will be fighting for control. You need to fight back. Fight until you are no longer able to control your body.

At that moment, when your body finally asserts control, try to be as aware as possible of the feeling. As you start to gulp in huge quantities of air, you will feel an acute sense of separation. Your mind and your body are two very distinct and different things. With very distinct and different needs. Your body is a machine. It needs tangible things. It needs food. It needs water. It needs air. Your mind, however, is something else entirely. And it needs quite different things. More than anything, it needs to understand. It needs to know. It needs, above all, to know the truth. It needs to understand the reality of your life.

It has been suggested, that 90% of long term happiness is not predicted by what happens to you, it is predicted rather by how you process those experiences. Perception is the issue.

I am sure that you have all heard the old saying, "When you are up to your ass in alligators, it is very difficult to remember that your original intention was to drain the swamp." This is even truer, when it comes to what is happening inside your head.

Unwanted and un-necessary thoughts often crowd out the ones you actually need to find your way to where you want to go. You stop thinking about what is happening and start simply reacting to it. Most of all, you start to worry. And that is such a waste of time. Worry is nothing more than praying for things you don't actually want. Certainly, things that you don't need.

It doesn't have to be this way. You can change it. All you need to do is this. There you are, lying on the couch/bed/floor, acutely aware of the separation of your mind and your body. Let your body do its thing. It knows what it needs. You work with your mind. Start to breathe slowly and evenly. Relax.

Now, with your eyes closed, "look" straight ahead. Picture a small point of light off in the distance. With each new breath, bring this point of light closer to you. Closer and closer, until it fills up your entire field of sight. A light so bright it is almost blinding.

In my experience of this, I have chosen to think of this light as plasma. You might choose to experience it as something else. I have a friend who "sees" this light as a doorway. It takes him to his special place. A place by a lake. Beside this lake, is a bench. When he is having a problem, either from the past or in the present, he invites the problem to come and sit down for a chat. In this place of safety, he is able to work through the problem and identify a solution.

It is important for you to keep an open mind as you look at this glowing ball of light. Be receptive to how your mind wants to interpret this. Your inner escape could take you anywhere. It could be anything. Just listen to your mind. Let it take you to your safe and special place.

Anyway, back to me. As this light grows, from a pindot in the distance, to a golf ball, to a tennis ball, to a beach ball, to a pulsing ball of pure and glowing white, thirty or forty or fifty feet across, I feel myself falling forward into it. I am completely surrounded by this ball of plasma.

Why plasma? I don't know, it just came to me. Plasma is the most abundant form of ordinary matter in the universe. It is the stuff of which stars are made. It is the substance of the most powerful force in the known world. It is what makes up the sun.

In this ball of glowing, bubbling plasma, I am safe. I can look, without fear, without anxiety, without prejudice, without preconceptions or misconceptions, at the problems I am facing. I can examine them. I can judge their validity. Their cause. Their effect. And I can choose to deal with them as I see fit.

Maybe it is something real. A real problem that requires a real solution. More often than not, however, it is a shadow from the past, masquerading as a problem of the present. This is when I get to use the most powerful weapon in my arsenal. Plasma.

I simply place this imposter of a problem in my sights and fire great big, glowing balls of plasma at it. I keep firing until it is completely covered in brilliant white light. And I watch it dissolve into nothing. It just fades away. The first time I tried this technique, I knew exactly what my target would be. I chose my hated ex-mother-in-law.

The thought of her had plagued me for too long. She had been living, rent free, in my head for long enough. So, I covered myself in plasma and pictured her standing before me in her twin-set and her pearls. I grabbed a big old handful of glowing white plasma and I let her have it.

It wasn't violent. It didn't hit her and cause her to explode into a thousand pieces. It was actually quite gentle. It covered her from the top of her head to the tips of her toes. And then she slowly dissolved. Soon, all that was left of her was an empty pair of shoes.

As bizarre as this may sound to you, and I am sure to many of you it does, it actually made a lot of sense to me. I had been tormented by the thoughts that surrounded her and my relationship to her. By her deception and the cruel way in which she had helped to engineer my abandonment.

I was filled with the negative thoughts and the negative emotions that had been caused by the circumstances of my breakup and divorce. These thoughts had been taking up too much valuable space in my head. It was time for them to go.

Every time these thoughts would return, every time she showed her frowning face, I would dive into the plasma and toss a little her way. Each time it took a little less. She would dissolve a little faster. Until she just stopped showing up. Today, I am free of her. Of the pain she caused. The pain I carried. She is gone and she is not coming back.

I still have my great big ball of plasma. I can get to it any time I need to. When a problem is forcing me to become unbalanced. To lose control. I go there and fire away. I burn away the power of the problem. I dissolve the negative emotions it has caused. In the aftermath, I am better able to see the problem more clearly. And I am able to make a better choice in how to resolve it. Or simply recognize that not all problems can be solved. Or even need to be.

However you choose to experience this Inner Escape, you will soon be able to exercise better control over how negative situations or negative people effect you. Once you have taken the "heat" out of any situation, you will begin to experience new insight into that situation.

You will be able to identify new and more effective solutions to your problems. Or, at least, a better understanding of what has caused them and why. Some issues will always remain unresolved. Some people never change. All you can do, is change how you let this affect you.

I sincerely hope that you try this technique and that it works as well for you as it does for me. For over a year, after having discovered this amazing technique, I kept it to myself. Foolishly, perhaps, I thought that others would mock me for suggesting it. Finally, I shared it with someone who was badly overstressed and was willing to try anything. And it worked. For them. It works for me. Maybe it will work for you.

But, even if it doesn't, it will prove one thing. You have a choice. Maybe it isn't this one, but it will be something else. Keep trying. Read more. Think more. Try more and different techniques. You will find one that works for you. Maybe it is meditation. Maybe it is just making your problem sit on an empty chair in the corner until it apologizes for the error of its way.

It really doesn't matter what you do, as long as you do something. It is in the action of taking control that the control actually exists. Avoidance and procrastination are the partners of failure. Never let them to be in control of you. Never let them take charge. Never stand by and helplessly allow them and their negativity to overwhelm you.

Right about now, you are probably saying to yourself, "Wow. What a bunch of crap. This can't possibly work. Certainly not for me." This is both understandable and more than half the problem. If you are like most people, your initial reaction to any new idea is doubt. Often, it is rejected out of hand. The universe offers you an opportunity and you take a pass. You say, "No". Actually, it is more like, "NO!" It isn't surprising really. It is probably the word you have heard most in your life.

It is estimated that you will have heard it at least 170,000 times before the end of your childhood. And who knows how many times since. It is estimated to be the very first word ever spoken in about 12% of children. So, why wouldn't you say it now?

The answer is simple. Because it won't get you anywhere. Certainly, it is unlikely to get you anywhere you might actually want to go. Instead, say "Yes". Give it a try. As silly or stupid as it might seem to you right now, give it a shot. If it doesn't work the first time, try it again. Change it to fit you. Maybe white just isn't your color. Okay, how about blue. Or pink. Or green. Maybe plasma isn't your thing. Try Jell-O chocolate pudding. Or purple poster paint. Get creative.

Also, get serious. This is your life we are talking about here. Is it worth feeling a little silly or self-conscious for a moment or two? Very little in this life works the first time we try it. Or the next. But keep at it. I promise that this will work. Or you will make it into something that does.

Inner Escape is a remarkable tool. I have suggested it to many people and the results have been profound. I have never had anyone who had given it a real try, come back to me and tell me that it had not worked. At least a little bit. I can't wait to hear from you.

A quick word about the next two chapters. The first, is about suicide, the following one about bullying. I encourage you to read them both. Don't just skip over them because these things have not been part of your life.

I guarantee you that someone in your life has dealt, or is currently dealing, with one or both of these issues. A huge part of living an Unstoppable life, is understanding those who aren't. And being willing to help them get past their own sticking point and start moving toward an Unstoppable life of their own.

CHAPTER 17

When doves cry

"How can you leave me just standing? Alone in a world so cold."

Prince was not talking about suicide, in this lyric he wrote back in 1984, he was singing about a failed love affair. But, isn't that one way to look at suicide? To see it as the tragic end to a love gone bad. The love, of course, is that of life. Just as romantic love fills your days and nights with joy and hope, so too does the love of life. And when that love, for whatever reason, ends, so too does that joy and hope.

Suicide is the tenth highest cause of death around the world. It is estimated that more than a million people a year take their own lives. What is even more disturbing, is that the numbers of attempted suicide are even higher.

Obviously, it is extremely difficult to arrive at any numbers that are even close to accurate, but the estimates are as high as 20,000,000 people a year who try to end their lives. That equates to almost 55,000 people per day. That means approximately six people either try to take their lives, or are successful at having done so, every minute of every day.

If there was any other disease that had such a staggering impact on our society, there would be a never ending series of telethons and walkathons and 5K runs and ice bucket challenges to find the cause and the cure. Unfortunately, there is no pathophysiology for suicide. There is no virus, or gene, or identifiable physical cause for suicide. Neither is there a vaccine, or surgery, or "magic bullet" that can cure it.

It is just another "one of those things" that almost nobody understands, or – to be honest – even wants to talk about. Suicide is our society's red-headed step child. We just sit there and hope that it never touches us or our family. But, it does.

I do not recall ever meeting someone, anyone, who has not been touched, in some way, by suicide. I would be willing to bet that the same is true for you. I can almost guarantee you that someone you know has either committed suicide, or tried to. A family member. A friend. The guy next door. Some girl at work. Maybe even yourself.

Suicide has been a part of my life for a very long time. You already know about that day on the balcony, but it wasn't my first time standing at the "edge" and looking into the darkness below.

The first time I actively thought about taking my own life, happened shortly after my arrival in Canada. I had made the move to this country out of basic necessity. I had very limited prospects in the UK. My school years, as you may recall, had been little more than a living hell. It had been very difficult to stay focused enough, due to the forces both inside and around me, to be even a little bit successful in my studies.

My test scores were abysmal. I was never going to receive a quality education and I wasn't sure that it would have made any difference. My future was looking as bleak as my past. Then something happened.

At the age of seventeen, I was offered the opportunity to immigrate to Canada. There was a program designed to bring new workers to the province of Ontario and I was accepted to be a part of it.

So, I left the dreary, rainy, depressing country of my birth and landed in one that was frozen solid. Twenty below and with snowdrifts taller than me. My first six months were a nightmare. I was not prepared, either physically or emotionally, to deal with the reality of living in Canada.

In addition to the freezing temperatures outside, the "chill" I was getting from prospective employers was just as bad. Nobody was even remotely interested in an uneducated, unskilled, unsophisticated kid from another country. Let alone one who twitched his way through the job interview.

I was just as unworthy and unwanted as I had been back home. So, I did what I had so relentlessly been trained to do as a child. I went to my room. I had a tiny room, with an even tinier television, and this became my world. I rarely ventured outside of this little space.

Why should I? Everybody I met rejected me. Everything I tried failed. Nothing was familiar. Everything was strange. I wasn't working. I wasn't living. All I was doing was lying in bed. And the only thing that came from that were bedsores. I couldn't even get up the energy to quit. I could have returned to England, but that would have meant getting out of bed.

Looking back at that time, I know now that I was suicidal. I do remember thinking about killing myself. Not actively, considering all the available ways to do so, or even passively, just lying there in my bed until I starved to death. No, I just lay there. I wasn't worried about what people would think. I knew that they wouldn't care. I certainly didn't. I wasn't concerned about the mess.

That would be someone else's problem. I wasn't worried about going to hell. I had been a student in the English school system. I am not actually sure why I didn't do it.

One day, I just got out of bed. The winter was ending. I had heard about a job that was available. I got on my feet and headed to the interview, where I got on my knees and begged for the job. I knew that I lacked education and experience. I knew that there was no logical reason that they should hire me. But, if they did, they would never regret it. I would work harder than anyone else. And I did.

The owner, a kind and benevolent man and another British expat, took pity on me and hired me to work in the mailroom of his growing import/export business. I made it a point to arrive an hour early every morning and leave every evening an hour late. I got on with it. My life. And every day, the nagging thoughts of suicide faded evermore away.

Did they go away completely? I thought they had. But, they hadn't. The depression and the despair that triggered those same thoughts during the first winter of my life in Canada, came rushing back in full force, as my beautiful young wife stood before me and told me that our life together was over.

The "black dog", as Winston Churchill called it, came back to live in my house. Depression became the strongest force in my life and I no longer had the strength to fight it.

So, I ended up on the balcony. As I told you earlier, the only thing I can point to for getting me to step back that night, was the thought of my poor Mother's beautiful face awash in tears. I know that this is what stopped me. I also knew that it wouldn't be enough. I needed help.

I went to the hospital first. In spite of all of my begging and pleading, and there was a lot, they turned me away. They did not have any room left in the psychiatric ward. This is, sadly, not unusual.

Overcrowded and understaffed, most of these facilities are simply unable to accommodate all who need them most. Need them now.

In the end, it was angels who saved me. Not the gossamer winged, harp playing kind – these two drank beer and swore as much as me. In desperation, I had called my friends Peter and Susan Bibby. Real names. Real friends. They didn't hesitate. They opened their hearts and their home to me and took me in. They saved my life.

They were there, when I needed to talk, and stayed silently in the background, when I needed to think. Peter and I would go for long walks along the beach. Our bare toes in the sand, I would pour out the miserable tales of woe to my friend. Not once did he judge me. Neither did he ever try to tell me what to think or how to feel. He just listened.

Slowly, I began to come back. To find my feet again. It didn't happen overnight. I can still remember the morning I found myself lying on their front lawn. I couldn't move. All of my systems had shut down. I was frozen in place. Blind. Mute. Deaf.

Oblivious to my surroundings. I lay there for most of the day. Until the color slowly started to come back into my gray world. Until I was able to get up and shuffle onward.

I am sure that you are familiar with the famous quote from Frederick Nietzsche, "That which does not kill you, makes you stronger." There has always been much debate about what this actually means, but for me it means this, "If I am still alive, I can still try."

This was never shown to be more true to me, than on the day I found myself walking onto a stage in Disney World. I had been invited back to speak to a large group of over twelve hundred travel industry professionals. They had seen me before and they wanted more. I could see them smiling in anticipation and delight. They knew what was coming.

As I walked out onto the stage, it suddenly hit me. Just how close I had come to missing all of this. These people. This day. I had come perilously close to not having any of this. My successful career. The respect and admiration of both clients and peers. My wonderful Doris. The true love of my life and the fantastic life we shared together. None of this would be happening. None of this would exist. If it had not been for one single backward step. And then another. And another. Until I was inside. Off the balcony.

Everyone who has ever considered suicide, has reached that point. Do you step forward? Do you step back? How do you know?

Stepping back is a choice. So too is stepping forward, but the difference is that by stepping back, you get to keep making choices. This may sound flippant to you, or even insincere, but I assure you that I am not joking. One of the saddest things about suicide, is that it means that the person was considering the options. They were actively looking for a solution to the situation. They made a choice.

Unfortunately, the choice they made, made all future choices impossible. It was their final choice. Making bad choices is part of life. We all make them. We all, hopefully, learn from them. We pick up the pieces and move on. We learn to make better choices.

But this choice, the choice of suicide, renders all of that moot. This will be the last choice they ever get to make. The last choice you ever get to make.

I am not assuming here, that you are suicidal. Not today. Not ever. But, if you are, or if you ever have been, you need to realize that you need help. And that help is all around you. There are telephone numbers you can call and websites you can click onto. There are facilities available to you. All of them staffed with competent, committed, concerned professionals. And, most of all, there are the people who love you.

They are there, even if you can't see them at the moment. Your friends. Your family. Even people with whom you work. If you are a religious person, there is someone at your church, or synagogue, or temple, or mosque. There are people all around you, who will come to your aid. All you need to do is ask.

Sometimes, however, asking for the help you need is the hardest thing to do. You need to get help, just to be able to ask for it.

Do not worry, there are ways to get past this. There are things that you can do. Simple things. Easy things. Private things.

If you are not ready to reach out for the help you need, it does not mean that you are lost. There is still much that you can do to get through this moment. This day. And tomorrow.

First of all, don't reach out. Reach in. Reach deep inside you to where all the pain and the fear lives. Stop pushing the pain away. Stop trying to make it stop. Instead, let it out. Let it wash over you. Let it flow through you. Cry. Weep. Scream. Swear.

It might be a good idea if you can find a nice quiet place where you can do this, free from interruption and audience, but, if not, just let it rip. GET IT OUT!

Now, try to remember to breathe. Slow. Steady. Deep. Fill your lungs until they feel like they will burst. Then blow it all out. Do it again.

Next, find one thing that is good in your life. Stop thinking about everything that is wrong, or bad, or not working. Try and think about one thing isn't any of those. Got it? Okay, now think about another. It doesn't matter what it is.

It could be a favorite food. Or a place you love to go. It could be a piece of music. Or a work of art. It could be your pet. Or a person who touched you in some way. Maybe it was that guy on the street who smiled at you for no reason. Just keep adding them up.

Now, if your tears have stopped and your heart has calmed, get up and go do something different. Something unexpected. Something you have never done before. Or something you love to do. If all that seems like it is too much, just go for a walk.

Get up. Put on your coat. Head out the door. Just keep putting one foot after the other. It doesn't matter where you are going. That isn't the point. Just being out there is the point. Keep walking. Keep breathing. Now, go home.

If this hasn't helped, even just a little bit, get out there and do it again. But, this time, try something else. Help the first person you meet. It really doesn't matter what you do. Hold a door open for them. Pick up something that they dropped and hand it back to them. With a smile.

That is something else you can do. Smile. Just keep smiling. Every time you pass any reflective surface; a mirror, or a store window, or even the side windows of a passing car; smile at yourself. Don't worry about what other people might think. They have their own issues. Just keep focused on you. And just keep smiling.

A recent article in Psychology Today speaks to the benefits of doing this. Even if you have to actually force yourself to do it. First of all, the action of smiling promotes our body's release of neuropeptides.

These little guys are the way in which our brain talks to itself. They are the tiny molecules that allow our neurons to communicate. Then, the neurotransmitters start to kick in. Dopamine, endorphins and serotonin are all released when a smile crosses your face. This helps you to relax. It slows your heart rate and lowers your blood pressure. But it doesn't stop there. Endorphins have even been shown to help to reduce pain and fatigue.

So, if you are sick and tired of being sick and tired, crack a smile. Better yet . . . laugh. The first guy who ever said, "Laughter is the best medicine" wasn't just talking through his rubber chicken.

But maybe there is an even better quote for this. Thich Nhat Hanh is an 88 year old Zen Buddhist monk, teacher, author, poet and peace activist who lives in a monastery in France. He goes right to the heart of this, when he said, "Sometimes your joy is the source of your smile, but sometimes your smile can be the source of your joy."

So, what have we got? Let out the pain. Let in the air. Get your butt outside and walk around. Help somebody. And . . . smile.

Will that take care of it? Will everything be better now? Of course not. I was just getting you ready for the one thing that will truly help you through this. For the one thing you need to get past this point in your life. What is this thing? As hard as this is going to be to do, you must find someone with whom you can talk about this.

The reason this is hard, for most people, is shame. Shame is such a crippling force in our lives and it isn't even something real. We make it up. A simple definition of shame, is when our actions do not reach up to the standards we set for them. We set for them.

Oh sure, we have lots of help in setting these standards, however unrealistic they may be, but we are the ones who accepted them. Parents. Teachers. The media. Religious beliefs. Political beliefs. Racial and ethnic stereotypes. All had their place in creating this, but we are responsible for making them so important they are about to kill us.

Whatever you do. However you can. Do not allow shame to prevent you from seeking out the help you need. I lived with shame for the most of my old life. It controlled and restricted my every waking moment. It made me weak and it made me vulnerable and it nearly killed me.

The hardest thing in the world for me to do, was the one thing that saved my life. I pushed past the shame and reached out my hand. I reached out to a friend. I asked for help and it was given. Kindly. Generously. Without condition or any thought of reward. It is why I am here today. And it is why I am telling you that it is what you need.

Remember the story of the in-flight oxygen mask. Put yours on first. Then help others. Because, if you don't do it in that order, nobody will survive. Get the help you need. Then be that source of help for the next person who needs it. You can do it.

I wish that I could tell you that it is easy to spot someone who is contemplating suicide. It isn't. We almost never know until it is too late. That doesn't mean we shouldn't try. Often the person who is actively considering suicide will seem perfectly normal. They will work extra hard at trying to appear that way. It becomes a huge part of their focus. It becomes their defense. And it is exhausting.

Albert Camus, the French Nobel Prize winning author, journalist and philosopher, wrote,

"Nobody realizes that some people expends tremendous amounts of energy, merely to appear normal."

It works. For a time. Eventually, however, the effort becomes too great. This will be when you are needed most. You will know when this is happening. You will know when a person needs you. Because you won't see them around. Time and again, people will say, "Oh, I was just leaving him alone. I thought that was what he wanted." Or, "She was always a private person. I didn't want to intrude."

Sometimes this is the right thing to do. These people aren't suicidal. They just wanted some time to themselves. But what about the other ones? The ones who do need your help. How do you tell the difference? Listen.

Listen to what they say. Is it always negative? Is it always sad? Is it always about how hard life is? Listen to your friends. Listen to your partner. Listen, most of all, to your children. The young are at the greatest risk today.

Children today see everything, but they don't understand any more of it than you do. In fact, they understand it less. They are at the greatest risk. And they have the fewest resources. So, talk to your children. Ask them how they are. Ask them how they feel. Ask them if everything is okay. Then shut up. And listen.

CHAPTER 18

Suffer the children

There is no way I can ever know your story. What you have experienced. How you have struggled. Your fears. Your pain.

All I can do, is share my story with you and hope that some small part of that story resonates with you. That you will be able to identify with my history and find some solace in the fact that these experiences are universal. Find some relief that your experiences have been shared, in so many ways, by so many others.

Unless you just happened to accidently open this book, for the first time, at this chapter, you already know about my experiences at school. How I lived in constant dread of each and every day spent among my classmates.

Every single day I knew, as I reluctantly walked to school, that I would be harassed, and embarrassed, and physically abused by at least one of the many bullies who took great delight in my constant suffering.

Oddly, it wasn't even the actual bullying that was so hard to bear; although I will never be able to adequately describe the pain and the humiliation of those brutal assaults; what tormented me most was the anticipation. I knew – I KNEW – that I was going to be bullied. I just never knew when. All I knew, was that it was only a matter of time. I spent every day of my youth with a big red bull's eye on my back. I walked those hallways with the measured tread of a condemned man on his way to the execution chamber. Dead man walking.

The only difference, is that I knew that I wasn't going to die. I wasn't going to be that lucky. There would be no relief for me.

If this is sounding a little melodramatic to you, it may because you are one of the lucky ones. You probably were never bullied. This is not a part of your history. Your story. If that is true, then I offer my sincere congratulations. This experience is not one that I would wish on anyone. And yet it happens to almost everyone.

Recent statistics suggest that 90% of students between the grades of 4 and 8 are victims of some type of bullying. This number drops as students move on to higher grades, but it does not stop.

Between ten and fifteen percent of high school students suffer ongoing bullying and those numbers are growing rapidly as cyberbullying becomes more common. It is an epidemic and it is getting worse. It is estimated that more than 160,000 students a day are skipping school to avoid being bullied.

But, why wouldn't they? Bullying happens once every seven minutes on the playground and once every twenty-five minutes inside the classroom. Yet, only one out of four teachers will intervene to put an end to it and even those who do, will only do so about 4% of the time. It has been reported that some teachers do not actually see anything wrong with bullying. They state that they believe that it helps to, "build character" and that the see no reason to interfere.

No reason to interfere? How about the fact that 10% of all high school students drop out because of bullying. Or worse. A study in Britain suggests that half of all teen suicides are the result of bullying. Suicide is the third leading cause of death among young people. And for every suicide, there are at least 100 attempts that failed.

Over 14% of high school students have contemplated suicide and almost 7% have tried to do so. The Centers for Disease Control has estimated the numbers of students who suffer death by suicide, at being in excess of five thousand a year. And those numbers are likely to get worse.

The victims of bullying are up to nine times more likely to commit suicide. With an estimated 30% of children living with the pressure of constant bullying – at school, on the playground, online, even at home – the number of them who may see suicide as their only solution will continue to grow.

One of the dilemmas associated with effecting any kind of real solution to bullying, is that it is almost impossible to get anyone to speak up about being bullied. The shame and embarrassment are too great. As I stated earlier, almost 90% of all children are bullied at some point in their lives and yet only a third of them will ever tell anyone about it. Not their parents. Not school authorities. Not the police.

Most of them won't even tell their friends. They try to hide away and hope that it will somehow, miraculously stop. Or, worse yet, they start to bully others. Perhaps in some vain hope that their bullies will see that they are just like them and stop.

In a way, it makes sense. Bullies are often among the most popular kids at school. Others look up to them and want to emulate them. So, they are very quick to join in when one of the "cool kids" starts to pick on a geek or a loser. This makes it very difficult to get a teacher, or any member of the school administration for that matter, to become either aware of the abuse, or willing to do anything about it.

It also discourages the other students who witness the bullying from trying to do anything to stop it. Certainly, no one ever came to my aid. Not at the worst of it. Not ever. What is worse, is I understand why.

By the time I was the age of ten, I had already become the object of relentless bullying by my classmates. Then, one day, a new target appeared. I will call him "David". David had just moved to our neighborhood and was starting classes in the middle of the school year.

This alone would have made him stand out, but our teacher made it even worse. David had, apparently, been bullied in his previous school and the teacher thought it advisable to inform the class of this and admonish us to make him feel welcome. He might as well have just stuck a huge "Kick me" sign on poor David's back.

Not that anyone would have needed much encouragement. David was a sad and sorry little creature. He was scrawny and unkempt but, what made it worse, was he liked to pick his nose and eat it.

Obviously, he had some sort of obsessive/compulsive disorder. He couldn't hide it and he couldn't stop. It was like blood in the water and the sharks came circling. They ravaged poor David. And I could not have been happier.

I know how horrible that must sound. It isn't that I disliked him. I didn't really know him. What I did know was this. As long as the bullies set their sights on him, they left me pretty much alone. My torment went from constant to occasional. And the relief was wonderful.

As I write this, I am overwhelmed with shame. Why didn't I do something? Anything? It isn't like I did not know what he was going through. I knew it all too well. I could have said something. I could have done something. I could have tried to stop it. But I didn't. I just stood there and watched. I didn't enjoy what was happening to him. It made me sick to see it.

I never joined in. I would have sooner chopped off my arm, than raise it to strike him. I didn't do anything to make his torture worse. But I never tried anything to make it less. Or stop. And for this I will always be ashamed.

I wish that I had possessed the courage to stand up for him, but I didn't really even have it to stand up for myself. In time, the bullies tired of tormenting David and returned their focus to me.

My two most committed and frequent abusers I will call "Simon" and "Malcolm". Simon like to abuse me verbally. He was an expert at coming up with new and inventive ways to insult and harass me. He was also remarkably adept at getting the other kids to form a circle around me and chant whatever vile diatribe he had created that day.

He was not, however, physical in his abuse. He was, however, the director of much of it. This is where Malcolm came in. Big and stupid. As mean as he was mindless, he followed S like a lumbering dog and attacked on command. I don't know if he would have ever beaten me, had it not been for Simon and his instructions, but beat me he did. Hard and often.

Of the two of them, Simon was by far the worst. A popular student, he was able to hide his contemptible nature behind the actions of others. Sure, he made up the repulsive rhymes the other students used to taunt me, but he would just fade away into the background, once his evil deed was done. He would stand to one side, smiling, as Malcolm beat the living crap out of me.

While he was often the mastermind behind the torment, he could seldom be seen to have done so. But I knew.

A few years ago, through Social Media, I was able to find him. He was living In Sussex and owned a small business. It was for this reason, that he had a page on LinkedIn. With a contact number.

So, I called the number and spoke with him. I told him my name and asked if he remembered me. He did. I asked if he remembered bullying me. That he also did. But, instead of apologizing, he launched into a long and vociferous defense of his actions. All children bully. It didn't mean anything. I told him he was wrong. It meant something to me.

Before he could start justifying his actions again, or hang up the phone, I told him that I forgive him. He was silent for a very long time. Then he did something surprising. First he apologized. Then he invited me to the upcoming class reunion at our old school.

I didn't go. I hold no fond memories of those days and I have no wish to see any of my old classmates. Those who had not actively bullied me, stood idly by and witnessed the abuse. They are not my friends. Neither is Simon.

We have never spoken again and I doubt that we ever shall. That part of my life is behind me. As are those people. All I carry forward from those days, are the memories. Mostly bad. I must say, however, that, as painful as those days were and the memories that remain of them, I cannot help but be grateful for them. In a very real sense, I would not be who I am, had they not been who they were. I learned a great deal from those experiences.

I learned, most of all, that when you are standing in the middle of a tempest and the storm is raging around you, the only thing that you can do is stand tall. Don't give up. Don't give in. Stand tall. Don't fall backward. Don't fall forward. Stand tall. Don't turn away. Don't run away. Stand tall. Face up to whatever is coming at you. You will make it through. The storm will end. The howling winds of doubt and fear will calm and you will survive. No matter how hard it may be to believe at the time. You will survive. You must. You have so much more to do.

One of the benefits – perhaps the only benefit – of being a bullying survivor, is that you know you have. In spite of all of the odds against it, you made it through and you got on with your life. Sure there are scars, but you made it, more or less, intact. But what about your tormentors. Whatever happened to the bullies?

A study in Britain showed that those who were bullies in grade school were more likely to have faced at least one count of criminal conviction by the age of twenty four. More than a third of them had multiple convictions by that age and continued to live a life of crime as time went on. Bullies in childhood became even greater bullies as they aged. But, why did they become bullies in the first place?

Those children who bully are often identified as angry, depressed, aggressive, hostile, and domineering individuals who show high levels of externalizing (acting-out) and hyperactive behaviors with little fondness for school and high conflict within friendships. Often they come from homes in which abuse is the norm. Physical. Emotional. Sexual. They are victims in their own lives. And they seek to ease their pain, by passing it on to others. Sadly, they continue to do this throughout their lives. The cycle is repeated.

I am one of the lucky ones. It didn't happen like that to me. Yes, I grew up in a troubled house. Yes, I was relentlessly bullied throughout my childhood. Yes, I felt weak and afraid for much of my youth. But, I didn't succumb. I am not really sure why.

Obviously, in part because of my Mother. Her love and support sustained me through much of this terrible time. She was not always able to protect me from the bullies. Most of the time, she didn't even know it was happening. And that was my fault.

Making the people in your life aware that you are being bullied is one of the most important and useful things you can do. As hard as it is to admit that you are a victim, you must. Nobody can help you if they don't know what is happening to you. Or to your children. You need to teach your children to stand up for themselves and, whenever possible, to stand up for others.

This does not mean that they should fight the bullies in any way that would endanger them physically, but they should be encouraged to seek out the help and support of any individual in a position of supervision or control. It has been shown that incidences of bullying activity are often stopped within ten seconds of any type of intervention.

Those at risk are identified and can be supported. Those causing the harm are also identified and can either be assisted in overcoming their impulses through counselling, or they can be removed from any position wherein they can continue to harass or assault their fellow students.

This is something that we can all do, whether we have someone in our life who is being bullied, or whether we just see the terrible toll this activity is having on our society. We can force school authorities to better monitor the behavior of their students. We can seek to bring about an open dialogue about the causes and the effects of bullying. And we can stand resolute in defiance to those who feel, for whatever feeble reason, that bullying is just a normal part of growing up.

Yes, I survived the bullies of my youth. As so too have many of you. We made it past that time and maybe we benefited, in some small way, from the experience. Maybe we became stronger. Maybe we learned compassion and humility. Maybe, if nothing else, we became aware of the problem and determined to find a solution.

Whatever the benefits we may claim we derived from our experiences, it is not enough to allow this type of behavior to continue. It isn't enough that those of us who survived, survived. We must make our survival have a greater meaning. We must speak out, whenever we can, about our experiences, our pain, the haunting memories we still carry with us, and the need for better means of prevention to this terrible problem.

Yes, there are lessons I learned on that schoolyard. I learned that words can hurt, almost as much as punches. I learned that feelings of mercy and compassion are not natural to all children. They must be taught to have them. I learned that it only seems easier to give up, than it does to stand up. I learned that bad times pass. And I learned that we have a responsibility to make our lives the very best we can, out of the pieces we have carried forward from the past.

One last story and I shall end this disturbing chapter. Many years ago, my Mother contacted me and told me that my Grandmother was in ill health and probably would not be with us for long.

She encouraged me to go and see her, before it was too late. She was trying to be kind. She knew that there had been problems between us – all families have their little ups and downs – but she was not fully aware of how badly I had suffered at the hands of her mother.

Thinking I was protecting her, I had never told my Mother the full extent of the abuse. It was my mistake. I realize now, I should have been honest with my Mother and told her about this. I should have had the courage to tell her and to make her believe me. Perhaps things could have been different. Perhaps it would not have ended the way it did.

I went to England. To my Grandmother's home. I sat in her small living room and I asked her, "Why?" Why had she done what she did? To such a small and helpless child. To someone who had trusted her. To someone who had done nothing wrong. Why had she beaten me so mercilessly? Did she regret it?

She sat there, this woman who had broken serving trays over my back, and looked at me in utter incomprehension. She didn't even know what I was talking about. One of the greatest horrors of my youth, this mean-spirited miserable old woman, and she didn't even remember.

I was stunned. I couldn't believe it. How could she not remember? How could this all have meant so little to her, when it meant so very much to me? I didn't get an apology. I didn't get any statements of regret. I didn't even get any acknowledgement of it even having happened. I did not get closure. I just stood up and walked away.

It didn't happen at first, but it did come to me eventually. Bullies don't recognize the enormous consequence of their actions. Their victims are nothing more to them, than a target for their rage and unhappiness.

Whereas the victim of a bully can remember every detail of each and every occasion of abuse, the bully can seldom remember it at all, let alone in any detail. We meant nothing to them. It was why they could do this to us. But not anymore.

The monsters of my past have faded away. The bullies are, for the most part, leading small and uneventful lives. My Grandmother is dead. My father as well. My ex-wife has moved on. My ex-mother-in-law has dissolved down to her shoes. And I am here.

And so too are you. You have made it. At least you have made it this far. The future is undetermined. That is up to you. To the choices you will make. To the rules you will write. You have the control now. You will use it as you see fit. My fervent hope, is that you use that control to make this world, or at least your part of it, a better place than when you came to be in it.

Bullies have always been a part of our reality. It would be foolhardy to assume that they will simply fade away and disappear. We can, however, make sure that they have less of an effect on the helpless and the meek. We can stand up to them, on other's behalf. We can become a powerful voice in this discussion. An Unstoppable force.

CHAPTER 19

All good things must begin

Well, this has been fun. At least it has been for me. And I sincerely hope it has been for you. If not actually fun, then I hope that it has been a little insightful and, more than a little, encouraging. This journey – the journey of life – is a challenging one.

At times hard and rocky. At times there will be steep hills and deep valleys. At times you will get lost along the way. At times you will need to stop and rest. At times you may need to ask a helpful stranger if he knows the way. I hope that I have been that "helpful stranger" for you. I hope that the story of my journey – one that is far from over – has truly been helpful.

I do not know where you are in your journey. I do not know where you have come from, or where you are going. Maybe you don't even know that. Maybe you are like Alice when she first entered into that strange and wonderful land beyond the looking glass.

"Alice: Would you tell me, please, which way I ought to go from here?
The Cheshire Cat: That depends a good deal on where you want to get to.
Alice: I don't much care where.
The Cheshire Cat: Then it doesn't much matter which way you go.
Alice: ...So long as I get somewhere.
The Cheshire Cat: Oh, you're sure to do that, if only you walk long enough."

Maybe that is where you find yourself today. Wanting to go. But not really knowing where. Not really caring where. You just want to be somewhere else. Maybe you just want to be someone else. And you can be. All you need to do . . . is begin.

As simple a thing as that sounds, I know how very difficult it can be. It certainly was for me. As I am sure it is for you. But it can be done. I did it. And if someone with all of the twitches and squeaks, fears and foibles, not to mention Bipolar and OCD, can pick up the pieces and put together a better life. Fuller. Happier. Unstoppable. Then so too can you.

It won't be easy. Not much that is truly worthwhile in this life is. It will take hard work and dedication. And I know how very difficult that is for some of you. Especially, if you are standing at the bottom of the hill. It seems like such a long way up. And you are so very tired.

This is how I felt, when I made the decision to start my own business. I was exhausted. Mentally. Physically. Emotionally. I was still reeling from my divorce. I was still haunted by my desire to leave this messy, troubling world behind. I had little money. And less energy. Now was not the time to be thinking about starting a business. Especially one that relied totally on me. I was a mess. What was I thinking?

I don't know that I can tell you exactly what I was thinking, but I can tell you where I was thinking it. In an effort to conserve my finances, I had decided to share an apartment. It was in my little room, that these ideas first came to me.

I remember sitting in front of my computer for days. Doing nothing. Just sitting there, staring at a blank screen. Arguing with myself. Should I do it? Should I not do it? How do I do it? How do I know if it will work? What the hell was "it" anyway? I don't know that I had any real idea of what I was doing. I just knew I had to do something. So I did.

Before I tell you what I did, I must remind you of something. In spite of my early success, as an independent teenager washing cars, I have always worked for someone. Some company. With a structure and framework. With rules and regulations. With expectations and rewards.

I had been successful inside these types of businesses. I took comfort in the order and stability they provided. It always gave me something to "fall back on". Not that I had ever actually needed it.

In every company for which I had worked, I soon became one of the best. I consistently outperformed my colleagues. I always met, and often exceeded, my quotas. I was almost always the top producer. In a way, that is quite easy to understand.

In a way, it was due to all of the abuse I had suffered as a child. In the face of that, someone on the phone saying "no" to me was hardly devastating.

Many of the salespeople with whom I worked had an almost pathological fear of rejection. Most people do. They would rather sit patiently by the telephone, waiting for someone to call them. Not me. Rejection was nothing new to me. I used to eat it for breakfast.

So, it was easy for me to pick up the phone and call fifty people a day. Or more. Sure, most of them were either disinterested or too busy to talk, but I was persistent. If they showed any interest at all, I would call them back. I would follow up on their questions and send them more information. I made serving their needs my priority. And it worked.

I arrived earlier and I stayed later. I worked harder. I faced up to the rejection and I surpassed everyone's expectations. Including my own. I had done that for so many companies. For so many years. And yet, here I was unable to move. Stuck in my bedroom. Staring at a blank computer screen. Unsure of how it would go. Unsure of how to even start. Something had to break. And it did. My fear.

Finally, my inner voice spoke up. "What are you waiting for?" it asked. "You have just gone through the wringer, mate. What could be worse than that?" The voice – my voice – was right. What was I waiting for? What was I afraid of? Enough is enough. It is time to get up and get on with it. So I did.

I didn't have much money, so an elaborate, sophisticated website was out of the question. Okay. Go with the basics. Just get something out there. I didn't have brochures, or CDS, or books like this. All I had was a telephone. And a voice. So, that is what I used.

I would get up at six o'clock in the morning, six days a week, and I would call. I would cold call. I would warm call. I would ask for referrals and then I would call them. I would spend sixteen hours a day on the phone. My ear would be red and swollen by the end of the day. I would be hoarse. Barely able to talk. So exhausted I would fall into my bed. Conveniently, it was only a couple of feet away. The next morning, I would get up and do it again. Then, the morning after that.

Before long, I was flying all over North America, meeting directly with those clients I had first approached over the phone. I had won their trust. Now I was winning their contracts.

In the first year, I did not earn much. Not compared to what I do today. But I was making money. And I was also making a difference. In my life. In the lives of others. I was speaking before ever larger groups of people. I was helping my clients to achieve their own Unstoppable goals.

I still work out of an office in my home. A much nicer home. And I still have a roommate. This time, however, it is not some smelly guy. It is the love of my life. My wife Doris. Together we get to share in everything that this journey has brought to us. The travel. The new experiences. The financial rewards. And, most of all, the happiness.

All because I finally said, "ENOUGH!" I got up off my backside and got on with my life. Or at least the search for it. I have done a lot of things in my life. Most of them to try and please others. But, I never was able to do enough. Be enough. To please them. Not all of them. I did make some people happy. Often at the cost of my own happiness. Too high a cost.

Finally, I said, "ENOUGH!", and I started to find ways to make me happy. At that point, something quite amazing started to happen. The happier I was, the happier I was able to make others.

It started on the phone. When I began to make sales calls, I was so happy just to have someone to talk to, I forgot that I was supposed to be selling. I would be sitting there, in my lonely little room, talking with someone hundreds, even thousands, of miles away and we would be becoming friends.

I was genuinely interested in them. In what they needed. In how I could help them. If I couldn't, I would tell them that and we would part on good terms. I could always call them back, if the situation changed. Often, I didn't have to. They would call me.

Over the many years, since I started my company in that little room, I have gone from "cold calls" to warm hugs. I have made friends all over the world. People I respect and admire. People who have added more to my life than I could have ever imagined.

For so much of my life, I simply assumed that I would end up miserable and alone. I had too many problems. Tourettes. Bipolar disorder. Anxiety disorder. OCD. I had been abused by family members. I had been tormented by bullies. I had been abandoned by those I loved. And ignored, or worse shunned, by strangers.

I had resigned myself to a life of less. I told myself I should be grateful for what I got. But I never was. I was never grateful for what I was grudgingly handed by others. For what I was told I deserved. I was never grateful for the scraps of a half-lived life.

I only began to feel gratitude, real gratitude, when I started to reach for what I truly wanted. When I stopped listening to the voices in my head. Those voices of others from the past. And started to listen to the voice in my heart. To my own voice. I began to make my own choices. I began to write my own rules. I still, and will always, do.

As I said at the beginning of this chapter, I don't know you. I don't know where you are. I don't know where you want to go. I don't know what you need. I don't know what you want. You are the only one who "knows". You are the only one who can answer any of that.

I can only assume, however, that you are still looking for these answers. Otherwise, I don't know why you have come this far in this book. Maybe it was just dogged determination to finish it. Good for you! That is a very valuable trait to possess. Often success, at anything, will go to the last person standing. This proves it could be you. It also proves something else. You are tired of listening to the voices in your head. That is why you have been willing to listen to mine. So, you are searching for the answers. For a way to change. But are you ready?

Most people look at life as an endless conveyer belt. Often, filled with problems and pain. More hard work. More long days. Stretching off into the distance. Bringing you one miserable day after another. It is no wonder they can never seem to get past this. This frustration. This disappointment.

The saddest thing of all, is that they have created this. They chose to look at their lives like this. If they chose, instead, to look at the conveyer belt in a different way, then their lives would also be different. If, rather than more failure and disappointment, they chose to see the belt as bringing more new and exciting opportunities – an endless supply of them – then their lives would be changed beyond recognition. Beyond their wildest expectations.

Maybe this is where you are. Facing the endless conveyer belt. If so, then I would doubt that it is bringing you much of what you truly want. Again, I assume that because you are still with me. I am very glad to have you here. I just don't want you to stay. It is very easy to get caught up in the search for answers. The real problem comes, when that is all you are doing. Looking for a direction, a path, often can become an end in itself. You can spend the rest of your life looking for your future. It is often so much easier than looking at your present.

I understand it. I do. But, I am warning you to avoid this trap. The more you procrastinate. The longer you put this off. The longer you keep searching for the "perfect" answer. The greater the chances are, that the years will simply pass you by. Time and opportunity will both be lost and you will be left with nothing but regret.

Kurt Vonnegut wrote, "Of all the words of mice and men, the saddest are, "It might have been." Please do not allow the shouldofs, wouldofs, and couldofs to be the sum total of your time here. You will regret it and you will hate your life because of it. There is, however, so much that you can do to change that. To avoid that.

Try this. Just sit down and ask yourself, "What is one thing I want to change in my life?" Write it down. Next to it, write down one way to make that change happen. It does not need to be the actual way you will affect the change, it is just a way to get you started. To get you thinking.

Write down a few things. It doesn't matter how silly or farfetched they might seem. Write them down. But be very aware of one thing. These have to be things that you could do. YOU. Not someone else. It isn't anyone else's job to fix your life. It is yours.

Also don't write down "winning the lottery".

That is not something you can ever possibly control. The only thing over which you will ever have any real control, is you. If you can find yourself, truly and completely, you can survive almost anything.

As I said, way back at the beginning, the problem is not what happens to us during our lives. It is how we allow that which has happened to affect us. And that is, and will always be, your choice.

So, make it. Choose to be in charge of your life. To be the engine of change. Start making choices. Start writing rules.

Not all of the changes will be positive. I promise you, they won't. People will notice. They might even fight you on it. That is actually a good thing. Change frightens a lot of people. They want everything to stay exactly the same. That is their comfort. If they are unhappy with you, it could very well mean that you are doing what is right for you. Which is likely to be wrong for them. You cannot allow this to stop you.

Far too many of us, change the way we are, the things we want and need, to accommodate those others around us. We don't want to make them unhappy. It is easier to be unhappy ourselves. Is that the life you have? Is that the life you want? No? Okay. So, you may upset some of the people in your life. You might even lose a few. But that is better than losing yourself.

Ask yourself, "Am I unhappy with anything in my life?" Write it down. Now, write down some ways in which you think you could change your life to become happier.

Again, don't worry about what you write. Be real. Be honest. But don't be concerned if it is something that you can do right away. Or ever. All you are doing, is getting in the habit of asking the right questions. And considering the boundless possibility that exists in the answers.

Maybe life isn't a conveyer belt at all. Maybe it is a roller coaster. Some days you are up. Some days you are down. Some days you are being thrown all around. But don't worry. You are not going to come off the track, or fall out of the car. Sure it can be scary. But that is all part of the ride. And it is, very much, worth the price of the ticket.

I was finally able, after much heartache and many false starts, to make for myself a truly Unstoppable life. So too can you. It all starts with a single step. A single choice. One new rule. Try.

No, I mean, TRY! Try something new. Try something different. Try something scary. Try something hard. If it doesn't work – and it probably won't – try something else. And keep on trying. Don't quit. The answers are out there for all of us. I have found some of mine and I am looking for the rest. I will never stop looking. This is actually fun.

As impossible as it might seem to you today, this will become your life. The endless search for answers. The constant quest for meaning. The restless journey toward your amazing future. And isn't that the point of being Unstoppable? Not stopping. Growing. Changing. Becoming stronger. Becoming whole. And sharing that with others.

Those you might love for the rest of your life. Those you might meet for only a moment. Be Unstoppable. Choose it. For yourself. For others.

Ask yourself this, "What is it I really want? To do? To be?"

Ask yourself this, "What is it that I am afraid of?"

Ask yourself this, "What is the weakness in me that is the
                              foundation of my greatest strength?"

Ask yourself this, "What am I waiting for?"

I have so many people I must thank for helping me to finally find myself. Those who were a negative influence in my life, are as valuable to me as those who provided a positive one.

I am grateful to the bullies, including my Grandmother, because they gave me the strength to endure. I am grateful to my fickle ex-wife because she showed me what love isn't and freed me to search for a love that is.

I am grateful to my Mother, for loving herself enough to leave something she knew and search for something she could only imagine. I am also, eternally, grateful for her boundless love and endless support. I honor her in everything I am and do. And, I am grateful to you.

You are why I wrote this book. As painful as some of it was, I am grateful for the opportunity to re-examine my journey. At where I was. At how far I have come. At how much farther I have yet to go. I am not done. Not hardly. I am nowhere near finished. There is so much left out there. To do. To feel. To be.

I invite you to take this journey with me. Hold my hand. Take a deep breath. Look, one last time, into the abyss. Look over the edge, into the darkness. Now, step back. Raise your head. Look into the warm and shining light above us. And smile.

Your journey begins today. With putting down this book. And getting on with your life. Your Unstoppable life.

Wait! I have one last quote for you. It is from Henry David Thoreau, an American author, poet, philosopher, abolitionist, naturalist, tax resister, development critic, surveyor, and historian. I know that he really didn't ever do much with his life, but he did say this:

"Never look back, unless you are planning on going that way."

Made in the USA
Charleston, SC
10 August 2015